ILLUSTRATED JOHN IN GREEK

GlossaHouse Illustrated Biblical Texts

ILLUSTRATED JOHN IN GREEK

GlossaHouse Illustrated Biblical Texts

Fredrick J. Long

T. Michael W. Halcomb

GlossaHouse
Wilmore, KY
www.GlossaHouse.com

Illustrated John in Greek
Copyright © 2018 by GlossaHouse, LLC

All rights reserved. No part of this work may be reproduced or transmitted in any form or by any means, electronic or mechanical, including photocopying and recording, or by means of any information storage or retrieval system, except as may be expressly permitted by the 1976 Copyright Act or in writing from the publisher. Requests for permission should be addressed in writing to the following:

GlossaHouse, LLC 110
Callis Circle
Wilmore, KY 40390

Bible. John. Greek. 2010.
 Illustrated John in Greek : GlossaHouse Illustrated Biblical Texts / Fredrick J. Long, T. Michael W. Halcomb, [Keith Neely, illustrator].– Wilmore, KY : GlossaHouse, [©2018].
xviii, 88 pages : color illustrations ; 28 cm. – (Accessible Greek Resources and Online Studies series. GlossaHouse Illustrated Biblical Texts. Bible)

Summary: The Greek text of the Gospel of John is set within colorful illustrations to represent narration, dialogue, monologue, and scripture quotations, together with a new English version by GlossaHouse translators. Text in English and Koinē Greek.

Library of Congress Control Number: 2018912737

ISBN: 978-1942697497 (pb)
1. Bible. John – Cartoons and comics. I. Long, Fredrick J., 1966- II. Halcomb, T. Michael W. III. Neely, Keith, 1943- IV. Title. IV. Series. V. Bible. John. English. 2018.

SBLGNT is the *The Greek New Testament: SBL Edition*. Copyright 2010 Society of Biblical Literature and Logos Bible Software [ISBN 978-1-58983-535-1]. The SBLGNT text can be found on-line at http://sblgnt.com. Information about the "Society of Biblical Literature" can be found at http://sbl-site.org and "Logos Bible Software" at http://logos.com.

The English translation of Mark used here, the GlossaHouse English Version (GEV), is original and has been created by T. Michael W. Halcomb and Fredrick J. Long.

The fonts used to create this work are available from linguistsoftware.com/lgku.htm. Illustrations and general illustration layout Copyright © 2006 Neely Publishing LLC.

Cover Design by T. Michael W. Halcomb
Book Design by T. Michael W. Halcomb, Fredrick J. Long, and Matthew R. Peterson
Illustration Design by Keith Neely

AGROS

Accessible Greek Resources and Online Studies

SERIES EDITORS
T. Michael W. Halcomb
Fredrick J. Long

AGROS

The Greek word ἀγρός is a field where seeds are planted and growth occurs. It can also denote a small village or community that forms around such a field. The type of community envisioned here is one that attends to Holy Scripture, particularly one that encourages the use of biblical Greek. Accessible Greek Resources and Online Studies (AGROS) is a tiered curriculum suite featuring innovative readers, grammars, specialized studies, and other exegetical resources to encourage and foster the exegetical use of biblical Greek. The goal of AGROS is to facilitate the creation and publication of innovative and affordable print and digital resources for the exposition of Scripture within the context of the global church. The AGROS curriculum includes five tiers, and each tier is indicated on the book's cover: Tier 1 (Beginning I), Tier 2 (Beginning II), Tier 3 (Intermediate I), Tier 4 (Intermediate II), and Tier 5 (Advanced). There are also two resource tracks: Conversational and Translational. Both involve intensive study of morphology, grammar, syntax, and discourse features. The conversational track specifically values the spoken word, and the enhanced learning associated with speaking a language in actual conversation. The translational track values the written word, and encourages analytical study to aide in understanding and translating biblical Greek and other Greek literature. The two resource tracks complement one another and can be pursued independently or together.

GLOSSAHOUSE ILLUSTRATED BIBLICAL TEXTS

TABLE OF CONTENTS

Introduction   x

ΚΑΤΑ ΙΩΑΝΝΗΝ (According to John)

Κεφ. Α΄ (Ch. 1)	2
Κεφ. Β΄ (Ch. 2)	7
Κεφ. Γ΄ (Ch. 3)	10
Κεφ. Δ΄ (Ch. 4)	13
Κεφ. Ε΄ (Ch. 5)	18
Κεφ. F΄ (Ch. 6)	22
Κεφ. Z΄ (Ch. 7)	29
Κεφ. Η΄ (Ch. 8)	34
Κεφ. Θ΄ (Ch. 9)	41
Κεφ. Ι΄ (Ch. 10)	45
Κεφ. ΙΑ΄ (Ch. 11)	49
Κεφ. ΙΒ΄ (Ch. 12)	54
Κεφ. ΙΓ΄ (Ch. 13)	59
Κεφ. ΙΔ΄ (Ch. 14)	63
Κεφ. ΙΕ΄ (Ch. 15)	65
Κεφ. IF΄ (Ch. 16)	66
Κεφ. ΙΖ΄ (Ch. 17)	68
Κεφ. ΙΗ΄ (Ch. 18)	69
Κεφ. ΙΘ΄ (Ch. 19)	74
Κεφ. Κ΄ (Ch. 20)	80
Κεφ. ΚΑ΄ (Ch. 21)	84

INTRODUCTION TO THE GREEK AND TRANSLATION OF THE GOSPEL OF JOHN

Illustrated John in Greek has been carefully designed from the initial editing of the Greek text of the SBLGNT edited by Michael W. Holmes, its translation, and its typesetting of the Greek narrative and speech among the beautiful illustrations by Keith Neely.

At the bottom of each page is the GlossaHouse English Version (GEV). This translation is fresh and fairly literal; we have attempted to preserve word order significance and accurately represent important features of the Greek text that are more emphasized and, therefore, more prominent. All of this was intended for the beginning student in mind, who may need help with Greek word meanings and understanding the significance of special constructions, like purpose, conditionals, and participles. In this translation work, we have applied current research on linguistics and Greek grammar, emphasis constructions, orality, performance, and social-cultural backgrounds. We have sought to strike a balance between trying to translate the import (as far as we can gather) of every sentence element but not "over" translating and moving into commentary. One must understand that every translation entails interpretation. We checked each other on a number of decisions, sometimes convincing the other of our particular views, sometimes not, on how best to translate some word, phrase, or construction. In the end, we are quite confident in the results, knowing that there will be things that have been missed and points for improvement and enhancement. Let us comment on various features and aspects of this translation.

Greek Word Order is preserved as long as it still makes "good" English sense, especially when some sort of prominence attends the fronted word order. For example, preserving the preverbal placement of adverbial modifiers often retains their prominence in Greek. Additionally, because of this, the beginning and intermediate student will often be able to readily recognize where the English glosses are for words and phrases.

Implied Words, most often objects of verbs and verbs, such as *it*, *him*, *them*, *is*, are often included in italics to help convey good English sense. The addition of such words was kept to a minimum. Seeing such words in italics may reveal to readers where the Greek text may co-relate verbs by sharing the same objects, which may contribute to understanding the tone or atmosphere of the event or its description.

Gender Inclusiveness is preserved as much as possible. Thus, the Greek word ἄνθρωπος is most essentially a *human being* (BDAG 81.1), although in many/most translations it is rendered as "a man" (which does not work in 1 Pet 3:4, which shows that ἄνθρωπος is not gender specific.[1] Typically, ἄνθρωπος is translated as "a person" or in the plural "people" especially when there is no gender specification intended from context, rather than "man/men." We find that using "person" helps readers away from unnecessary gender bias; so, when Jesus encounters the man at the pool in John 5, the man is simply introduced as "a person there" (5:5), and in the end, it is his "personhood" restored and not his manhood (5:9). This decision also affects the many instances of Jesus as "the Son

---

[1] I am indebted to Andy Barlow for alerting me to this example.

of Man" (likely from Dan 7:13), which we rendered "the Son of Humanity." We believe that the title "the Son of Humanity" signifies Jesus's role as been given the right to judge, to both represent humanity and to deliver humanity (see John 5:27).

Every Particle or **Conjunction** has been translated, including the very frequently occurring instances of καί and δέ. This has been a common fault of modern English Translations in general not to, sometimes with important interpretations at stake. Καί is marked +continuity but also +additive. When used adverbially as ascensive καί, this indicates additive emphasis and is often translated "also" or "even." Otherwise, καί is translated "and." The conjunction δέ is marked +new development, but can be used with contrasts (very context specific), but otherwise was translated so as to indicate movement in narrative. Thus, the following words have been used: *well*, *thus*, *moreover*, *additionally*, *but*, *so* (used in consequential narrative development is implied contextually), and occasionally *and*. The conjunction ἵνα, when indicating purpose, we have attempted to always render as *in order that*, which distinguishes it from result clauses (*so that*) or content clauses (*that*). However, there are instances where the sense of purpose, content, or result (much less common) were hard to distinguish (e.g., requests), so ἵνα may be translated simple as *that*. Finally, for purpose statements, since the notion of intention is pivotal, the English helping verb *would* is much preferable to *might* or *should*; this should be a corrective to learning that the subjunctive is a mood of possibility and can be translated with "might."

Verb Tenses in the Indicative Mood are translated somewhat consistently, with the most variation occurring with the Historical Present and the Imperfect. In light of the ongoing debate on the significance of the Greek verb and verbal aspect, we have taken a fairly conservative approach. The imperfective verbal aspect (incomplete, in progress, internal) occurs in the Present and Imperfect Tenses; perfective aspect (complete or completed, external) in the Aorist Tense; stative/resultative aspect (complex action with effects) in the Perfect and Pluperfect Tenses; and future aspect (expectation) in the Future Tense.[2] Our goal was to allow transparency in the translation; it is not that we think the translations are the best way to translate this or that verb in this or that context in every instance, but rather we wanted transparency in the English tense translation to the underlying Greek tenses, in order to facilitate observation, and further research and conversation. That being said, however, it is our current understanding that the augment in the Indicative moods marks past time, or possibly only remoteness; however, such remoteness would in narrative most often indicate past time.

Generally, we translated the **historical present** tense as "continues …ing," or "keeps …ing" etc. Thus, for example, translating λέγει "he says" (generically) depended on context: Sometimes we translated as inceptive ("he begins saying…"), sometimes as continuative ("he proceeds saying), sometimes as progressive ("he kept saying"), and sometimes as simple present ("he says…"). Similarly, translated the **imperfect indicative**, but placed into past time conception, as "kept …ing"

---

[2] For the traditional designations of imperfective, aoristic, and perfective, see David Alan Black, *It's Still Greek to Me: An Easy-to-Understand Guide to Intermediate Greek* (Grand Rapids: Baker, 1998), 96–97. On the discourse relation of the tenses in the Indicative mood, see Long, *Koine Greek Grammar*, 125–27, 245–47.

or if beginning a unit, "began ...ing." Thus, for example,

> John 4:31 Ἐν τῷ μεταξὺ <u>ἠρώτων</u> αὐτὸν οἱ μαθηταὶ λέγοντες· Ῥαββί, φάγε.
> John 4:31 In the meantime, the disciples <u>kept begging</u> him, saying, "Rabbi, eat!"

Cultural Idioms were carefully considered.

- Thus, the "Feast" of Passover is capitalized (e.g., 4:45; 6:4; 12:12, 20, etc.).
- Ῥαββί is translated as "My Master" or "Our Master" to avoid anachronism, since Rabbis as we now understand them were a much later development. Also, to avoid confusion with "Lord" (κύριος) and "teacher" (διδάσκαλος); additionally, this is closer to the Hebrew that has the first-person pronominal suffix *Rabb-iy*. When Jesus is addressed as Ῥαββί by a group (e.g., 9:2; 11:8), then Ῥαββί is translated "Our Master." However, in 20:16 when Mary recognizes Jesus, we have preserved the Aramaic Ραββουνι as "Rabboni" since this is immediately translated as "Teacher."
- "The Galilee" is thus translated (see 1:43 *passim*), which is in keeping with historical practice, even up to this day. The same does not apply to "Judea" or "Samaria," etc.
- Based on contextual indicators, we have translated Ἰουδαῖοι (typically glossed "Jews" or "Judeans") as "Jewish officials" in every instance where the substantive adjective signifies the group as agents. Often, this occurs in the nominative plural. John's Gospel presents this group as the main group questioning and challenging Jesus, beginning right away in 1:19 (see 2:18, 20; 5:9, 15–16; 6:52, etc.). Also, we choose not to translate this as "Judean" based in part because John distinguishes "the Judean land" (3:22), which contrasts with 1:19 where Jerusalem is singled out after mention of "the Jewish Officials." Hence, "Judean" cannot always be glossed for the term Ἰουδαῖος. John 7 also illustrates this distinction quite clearly (esp. 7:1). Then in John 11–12, readers are introduced to two groups of Jews. First are "many from the Jews" (πολλοὶ ἐκ τῶν Ἰουδαίων, 11:19) who console Mary and Martha at the loss of their brother. These Jews remain active on the scene (11:31, 33, 36) and believed in Jesus (11:45). Second, another group is introduced (12:9) who likewise believed in Jesus (12:11). These two "believing" groups are to be distinguished from the Jewish officials who want to kill Jesus (11:8, 53) such that Jesus could no longer walk among them (11:54).
- A devil or an adversary? In 6:70, we have chosen to render διάβολός as "adversary" (see BDAG s.v.) in contrast to with the English translation tradition.
- Various time constructions with αἰών or αἰώνιος:
    - ζωὴν αἰώνιον is translated as "everlasting life" rather than "eternal life" (3:15 *passim*).
    - εἰς τὸν αἰῶνα is translated as "into the age to come" (11:26, 12:34, 13:8, 14:16).
    - ἐκ τοῦ αἰῶνος is translated as "from the beginning of time" (9:32).

Various Types of Marked Constructions that convey some sort of emphasis were translated in such a way as to indicate their importance.[3] Below is a brief accounting of these constructions, although this brief list does not nearly exhaust the different ways that Greek can indicate emphasis and give more prominence to sentences elements or discourse features; these latter, nevertheless, are hard to translate and often would have required extensive explanation. More work is needed here; the following constructions were fairly clear to translate:

- <u>Redundant nominative personal pronouns</u> emphasize the subject, since the verbal endings are already mark subject person. Such redundancy is indicated by adding *–self* to the subject. So, in 3:11 one will find <u>Σὺ</u> εἶ ὁ υἱὸς τοῦ θεοῦ "You <u>yourself</u> are the Son of God!"
- <u>Fronted genitives</u> place more stress on the noun or pronoun possessing the head noun. Thus, in 4:34 αὐτοῦ τὸ ἔργον is translated "this work of his" to emphasize the fronted genitive referring to God's work.
- <u>Adjectives in the second attributive position</u> are more prominent than those in the first position. Consider this example with <u>τὸν ἀληθινόν</u> modifying τὸν ἄρτον:

  John 6:32 εἶπεν οὖν αὐτοῖς ὁ Ἰησοῦς· Ἀμὴν ἀμὴν λέγω ὑμῖν, οὐ Μωϋσῆς δέδωκεν ὑμῖν τὸν ἄρτον ἐκ τοῦ οὐρανοῦ, ἀλλ' ὁ πατήρ μου δίδωσιν ὑμῖν τὸν ἄρτον ἐκ τοῦ οὐρανοῦ <u>τὸν ἀληθινόν</u>·

  John 6:32 "Therefore, Jesus said to them, "Amen! Amen! I keep saying to you, Moses has not given to you the bread from heaven, but my Father is giving to you the bread from heaven *that is* true."

- <u>Emphatic negation</u> with οὐ μή is often rendered *never ever* to capture the emphasis. Depending on the attending constructions, this is not always possible.
- <u>Attention Getters</u> such as Ἴδε ("Look" or "See") and Ἰδού ("Behold") were thus differentiated.

  John 11:36 ἔλεγον οὖν οἱ Ἰουδαῖοι· Ἴδε πῶς ἐφίλει αὐτόν.
  John 11:36 The Jews, therefore, were saying, "See how he was loving him!"

  John 12:15 Μὴ φοβοῦ, θυγάτηρ Σιών· ἰδοὺ ὁ βασιλεύς σου ἔρχεται, καθήμενος ἐπὶ πῶλον ὄνου.
  John 12:15 "Fear not, daughter of Zion! Behold, your King comes, sitting on a donkey's colt."

- <u>Rhetorical questions</u> that indicate wither an expected affirmative or negative response are

---

[3] For a discussion of the issues, see Stanley E. Porter, "Prominence: An Overview," in *The Linguist as Pedagogue: Trends in the Teaching and Linguistic Analysis of the Greek New Testament,* ed. Stanley E. Porter and Matthew Brook O'Donnell; New Testament Monographs 11 (Sheffield: Sheffield Phoenix, 2009), 45–74. On marked, emphasized, and prominent features described here and others not described, see Fredrick J. Long, *Koine Greek Grammar: A Beginning-Intermediate Exegetical and Pragmatic Grammar* Accessible Greek Resources and Online Studies (Wilmore, KY: GlossaHouse, 2015) and idem, *2 Corinthians: A Handbook on the Greek Text*, Baylor Handbook on the Greek New Testament (Waco, TX: Baylor University Press, 2014).

worded in such a way as to indicate as much, and then the response is placed within parentheses with an exclamation mark (No!) or (Surely no!) or (Surely yes!). Remember the rule of MNOP: μή or μητί expects negative answer (No!) and (Surely no!), respectively, whereas οὐ or οὐχί expects a positive answer (Yes!) and (Surely yes!), respectively. To see these rhetorical questions clearly in the English translation conveys the tone of disappointment, correction, surprise, or confrontation. For example,

John 4:29 Δεῦτε ἴδετε ἄνθρωπον ὃς εἶπέ μοι πάντα ὅσα ἐποίησα· μήτι οὗτός ἐστιν ὁ χριστός;
John 4:29 "Come, see a person who spoke to me all things, how much I did! This man isn't the Christ, is he? (No, he couldn't be!)"

o Recitative ὅτι is an optional phenomenon; direct speech may or may not be introduced by ὅτι. When ὅτι does occur, it likely sets off the statement for some discursive, pragmatic reason. Stephen H. Levinsohn proposes that it may help signal the culmination of an argument or, in John's Gospel, the explanation of previous teaching.[4] Most essentially, it would seem that recitative ὅτι is marked + prominence for introducing important direct speech, which may happen (often) to culminate a unit or explicate teaching. We have chosen to indicate the presence of recitative ὅτι by translating it with a near demonstrative pronoun "this: …", because "this: …" sets off and anticipates what follows formally in English. For example, consider 8:24a:

John 8:24a εἶπον οὖν ὑμῖν ὅτι ποθανεῖσθε ἐν ταῖς ἁμαρτίαις ὑμῶν·
John 8:24a Therefore, I said to you this: 'You will die in your sins;

Another intriguing example is seen in 4:1 in which the ὅτι sets off what was "heard" about Jesus. Typically, it is explained that indirect discourse like this retains the tense of the original statement; yet, this translation helps to convey this very sense present in the Greek idiom.

John 4:1 Ὡς οὖν ἔγνω ὁ Ἰησοῦς ὅτι ἤκουσαν οἱ Φαρισαῖοι ὅτι Ἰησοῦς πλείονας μαθητὰς ποιεῖ καὶ βαπτίζει ἢ Ἰωάννης
John 4:1 Therefore, when Jesus knew that the Pharisees heard this: "Jesus makes and baptizes more disciples than John"

o The Verb ἀποκρίνομαι, typically glossed as *I answer*, is used to mark participants taking back control or controlling the conversation. Stephen H. Levinsohn suggests that the use of the verb marks an attempt to control or take over the conversation.[5] Therefore, we have chosen the

---

[4] Stephen H. Levinsohn has been interested in describing the discourse pragmatic function of ὅτι in narrative with verbs of saying (*Discourse Features of New Testament Greek: A Coursebook on the Information Structure of New Testament Greek*, 2nd ed. [Dallas: Summer Institute of Linguistics, 2000] ch.16). His conclusions are that in John and Luke-Acts such explicit use of ὅτι occurs at the culmination of a unit or sub-unit, i.e., the ὅτι will "signal that the quotation it introduces culminates an argument" (269). He also notes that in Luke's and John's Gospel the statement Ἀμὴν ἀμὴν λέγω ὑμῖν/σοι "Truly, truly I say to you," when followed by ὅτι, is used to ex-plicate previous teaching. See also Levinsohn, "Ὅτι Recitativum in John's Gospel: A Stylistic or a Pragmatic Device?," *Working Papers of the Summer Institute of Linguistics*, University of North Dakota Session 43 (1999): 1–14. Online: http://www.und.edu/dept/linguistics/wp/1999Levinsohn.PDF.

[5] Levinsohn, *Discourse Features*, 231–35; Long, *Koine Greek Grammar*, 356–59.

gloss, *I answer back*, as is reflected in the translation. Such a decision augments one's understanding of the agonistic environment of challenge-riposte, and statement and response back, that this verb illustrates so well.

- o <u>The Affirmative ἀμήν *Amen!*</u> we have understood as a stand-alone or clause final particle of affirmation that is predominantly backward pointing.[6] Such an understanding comports with its liturgical backward referencing in Hebrew Scripture to affirm what has been said (BDAG 53.1a).[7] This understanding of ἀμήν differs quite significantly from the typical translation of Jesus's usage with verbs of sayings as "Truly, truly I say to you…" that points forward at the "beginning a solemn declaration but used only by Jesus" (BDAG 53.1b.). Thus, we have translated ἀμήν ἀμήν "Amen! Amen!" as affirming what has just been said, believed, or done.[8]

Punctuation decisions are difficult. For imperatives and statements involving feeling, exclamation marks were used to help capture that tone and feeling. Also, we felt compelled at times to show different punctuation and wording than found in the SBLGNT; such decisions are interpretive. Below are examples from the John 1–12 to illustrate where and why we made these decisions.

1:15—We understood this verse not to be an aside in parentheses (*pace* SBLGNT).
1:16—We have removed the comma in ἐλάβομεν, καὶ…
1:19—We added a comma to show focus by use of a redundant personal pronoun in the phrase "You, who are you?" (Σὺ τίς εἶ; cf. 1:21) which differs from "Who are you?" of 1:22 (Τίς εἶ;).
1:24—In our translation, we changed a period to a comma.
2:23 and 5:8—These are examples where we have commas in English that are not in the Greek.
3:2, 11—We have changed the punctuation so that "Amen! Amen!" serves to affirm the previous statement as was common idiom. This same practice has been followed in every subsequent instance. See the discussion immediately above.
4:1–2—We removed both em dash symbols (—) and placed 4:2 inside parentheses.
4:5—Although normally raised dots are equivalent to colons or semi-colons., we used a period.
4:35—two quoted statements added
4:35–36—We moved the ἤδη at the end of 4:35 to the beginning of 4:36 (so also NA[27-28]).
4:37—We understood the ὅτι as indicating indirect rather than direct discourse, so the Greek text Ἄλλος has been changed to lower case ἄλλος. Verse 37 is commentary on verse 36 rather than introducing a direct quotation.

John 4:37 ἐν γὰρ τούτῳ ὁ λόγος ἐστὶν ἀληθινὸς ὅτι Ἄλλος ἐστὶν ὁ σπείρων καὶ ἄλλος ὁ θερίζων·
John 4:37 For in this way, the saying is true that one is the one sowing and another is the one reaping.

---

[6] This suggestion was first made by T. Michael W. Halcomb who has researched this extensively and presented this research at the Society of Biblical Literature annual meeting.

[7] For a discussion and summary of Halcomb's research and presentations in this area, see Long, *Koine Greek Grammar*, 279–80.

[8] This view and translation of ἀμήν as "Amen!" is implemented in our book, *Illustrated Mark in Greek*, reprinted in GlossaHouse Illustrated Biblical Texts (Wilmore, KY: GlossaHouse, 2014, 2018).

5:4—We added this verse following the Byzantine Tradition that the SBLGNT does not have.

5:45a—We have changed the punctuation to indicate a rhetorical question: μὴ δοκεῖτε ὅτι ἐγὼ κατηγορήσω ὑμῶν πρὸς τὸν πατέρα; "You are not supposing that I myself will accuse you before the Father, are you? (No!)" This logic seems to make better sense of the conversational flow.

6:20—We place a period after "I am" instead of a comma.

6:22—We placed a period at the end instead of a raised dot.

6:65—We understand the ὅτι to be Jesus's summary of his teaching. Thus,

> John 6:65 καὶ ἔλεγεν· Διὰ τοῦτο εἴρηκα ὑμῖν ὅτι οὐδεὶς δύναται ἐλθεῖν πρός με ἐὰν μὴ ᾖ δεδομένον αὐτῷ ἐκ τοῦ πατρός.
>
> John 6:65 And he continued saying, "On account of this, I have said to you this: 'No one is able to come to me, unless it should be given to him from the Father.'"

7:6–7—The comma after πάρεστιν was changed to a raised dot in order to indicate two independent statements. Ὁ καιρὸς ὁ ἐμὸς οὔπω πάρεστιν· ὁ δὲ καιρὸς ὁ ὑμέτερος πάντοτέ ἐστιν ἕτοιμος. So, similarly, in 7:7 the comma after ὑμᾶς, has been changed to a raised dot.

7:20—The raised dot in Δαιμόνιον ἔχεις· has been translated with an exclamation point, since it seems to be a charge against Jesus: "You have a demon!"

8:15 and 8:23—The commas after κρίνετε, and ἐστέ, we changed to raised dots indicating a semicolon in English

8:25—We changed the ὅ τι to a recitative ὅτι and thus also changed the semicolon (which would indicate a question) to a period (indicating this is a statement). Thus, εἶπεν αὐτοῖς ὁ Ἰησοῦς· Τὴν ἀρχὴν is repunctuated as εἶπεν αὐτοῖς ὁ Ἰησοῦς τὴν ἀρχὴν ὅτι· We understand τὴν ἀρχὴν here to be an idiom to mean "to begin with" (see "ἀρχή" LSJ, 252.1.c).

9:3-4—We removed the period and replaced with a comma, which causes the ἵνα clause to be a subordinate purpose clause going with 9:4, rather than 9:3.

10:29—We have not accepted the SBLGNT's choice of ὅ but agreed with the NA28's ὅς. Thus,

> John 10:29 ὁ πατήρ μου ⌜ὃ δέδωκέν ⌜μοι ⌜πάντων μεῖζων⌝ ἐστιν, καὶ οὐδεὶς δύναται ἁρπάζειν ἐκ τῆς χειρὸς τοῦ ⌜πατρός.
>
> John 10:29 My Father, who has given *them* to me, is greater than all, and no one is able to be snatching *them* out of the Father's hand.

10:38—We added a second comma after μὴ πιστεύητε,... Thus,

> John 10:38 εἰ δὲ ποιῶ, κἂν ἐμοὶ μὴ πιστεύητε, τοῖς ἔργοις ⌜πιστεύετε, ἵνα γνῶτε καὶ ⌜γινώσκητε ὅτι ἐν ἐμοὶ ὁ πατὴρ κἀγὼ ἐν ⌜τῷ πατρί⌝.
>
> John 10:38 But if I am doing *them*, although you do not trust me, trust the works, in order that you would know and understand that the Father *is* in me and I myself *am* in the Father."

11:13—We changed the period in the middle of the verse to a raised dot (·) to indicate a semicolon.

11:56—We changed the punctuation, Τί δοκεῖ ὑμῖν; ὅτι... to Τί δοκεῖ ὑμῖν ὅτι...

12:16—We understood as a parenthetical remark and we added parentheses to denote that.

Finally, a restored **Koine Era Pronunciation (KEP)** is recommended to help hear original rhyming, cadence, alliterations, consonance, and other sound patterns.[9] Below is an overview of KEP.

ALPHABET				VOWEL PAIRS		
Letters	Transliteration Value	Pronunciation (Approx. English Sound)	Examples	Letters	Transliteration Value	Pronunciation (Approx. English Sound)
Α, α	A, a	ah – tor<u>ah</u>	λαμβάνω lam<u>v</u>anō	αι	ai	ai (= eh) – s<u>ai</u>d
Β, β	V, v	v – <u>v</u>et	λαμβάνω lam<u>v</u>anō	αυ	av, af (before β, δ, γ, λ, μ, ν, ρ, ζ)	av – a<u>v</u>ocado af – w<u>af</u>t
Γ, γ	Y, y – before ε, ι, ει Gh, gh – before other vowels	y – <u>y</u>et gh – <u>gh</u>ost (but a bit softer)	ἅγιος a-<u>y</u>iōs ἀγαθός a<u>gh</u>athōs	ει	ei	ee – b<u>ee</u>t
Δ, δ	Dh, dh or Th, th	dh – <u>th</u>e (no good English equivalent) th – <u>th</u>e	διά <u>dh</u>ia, <u>th</u>ia	ευ	ev, ef (before β, δ, γ, λ, μ, ν, ρ, ζ)	ev – <u>ev</u>ery ef – l<u>ef</u>t
Ε, ε	E, e	eh – mikv<u>eh</u>	σέ, s<u>eh</u>	ηυ	āv, āf (before β, δ, γ, λ, μ, ν, ρ, ζ)	āv – ā<u>v</u>ery āf – sāfe
Ζ, ζ	Z, z	z – <u>z</u>oo	ζῶον, <u>z</u>ōon	οι	oi	like "eew" in "jus" of French "au jus"
Η, η	Ā, ā	āy – p<u>ay</u>	μή, m<u>āy</u>	ου	ou	ou – c<u>ou</u>p
Θ, ϑ	Th, th	th – <u>th</u>ink	θεός, <u>th</u>eh-ōs	υι	ui	iy – ter<u>iy</u>aki
Ι, ι	I, i Y, y (in Hebrew names in Greek)	ee – b<u>ee</u>t y – <u>y</u>es (often will begin words)	τίς, t<u>ee</u>s Ἰησοῦς <u>Y</u>āy-sous			
Κ, κ	K, k	k – <u>k</u>ey	καί, <u>k</u>eh	CONSONANT PARIS		
Λ, λ	L, l	l – <u>l</u>eg	λέγω, <u>l</u>egō	γγ	ng	ng – ha<u>ng</u>
Μ, μ	M, m	m – <u>m</u>ad	μέν, <u>m</u>ehn	γκ	nk	nk – du<u>nk</u>
Ν, ν	N, n	n – <u>n</u>o	νῦν, <u>n</u>eew<u>n</u>	γχ	nkh	nkh – a<u>nkh</u>
Ξ, ξ	Ks, ks	ks – boo<u>ks</u>	ξένος, <u>ks</u>enōs	γξ	nks	nks – tha<u>nks</u>
Ο, ο	Ō, ō	o – g<u>o</u>	πρός, pr<u>ō</u>s	μβ	mv	mv – hu<u>mv</u>ee
Π, π	P, p	p – <u>p</u>eek	παῖς, <u>p</u>ehs	ντ	nt	nt – a<u>nt</u>, or nd – a<u>nd</u>
Ρ, ρ	R, r	r – rim (trill/roll)	ῥίζα, <u>r</u>iza			
Σ, σ, ς	S, s	s – <u>s</u>it	σοῦ, <u>s</u>ou			
Τ, τ	T, t	t – <u>t</u>ip	τίς, <u>t</u>ees			
Υ, υ	Y, y V, v – in diphthongs following α, ε, η (i.e. αυ, ευ, ηυ)	eew – au jus (cf. οι) av – a<u>v</u>ocado (αυ) ev – <u>ev</u>ery (ευ) āv – ā<u>v</u>ery (ηυ)	κύριος, k<u>y</u>r-iōs For examples, see diphthongs at right.			
Φ, φ	F, f (or Ph, ph)	f – <u>f</u>it	φάγε, <u>f</u>a-yeh			
Χ, χ	Kh, kh (or X, x)	kh – bac<u>kh</u>oe (guttural)	χάρις <u>kh</u>aris			
Ψ, ψ	Ps, ps	ps – <u>ps</u>alm	ψώρα, <u>ps</u>ōra			
Ω, ω	Ō, ō	o – g<u>o</u>	ᾠόν, <u>ō</u>ōn			

Note: While the rough breathing mark is denoted in writing (e.g., Ἡ, ἡ), there is no "rough breathing" sound (the voiced "h" in "ha" or "help") articulated in the Koine Era Pronunciation. This is because aspiration (rough breathing) had fallen out of use hundreds of years prior to the Koine-Hellenistic era. In spite of this fact, Erasmian pronunciation continues to use rough breathing.

---

[9] For a discussion, see Long, *Koine Greek Grammar*, ch. 2. This overview, slightly edited, first appeared in our book *Illustrated Mark in Greek*, ix.

The most essential differences when transitioning from Erasmian pronunciation to KEP are these:

Vowels and Vowel Pairs (Monophthongs and Diphthongs)

ε = "eh" as in "b<u>e</u>t" (**not** "ah" or "[h]ay" [long "aaa"])
αι = "eh" as in "b<u>e</u>t" (**not** "eye/ I").
Thus, ε = αι in KEP. So, καί = "keh"

η = "ay" (long a) sound **not** "eh"

ι = "ee" sound
ει = "ee" sound

υ = "eew" as in ewe or au <u>jus</u> (French)
οι = "eew" as in ewe or au <u>jus</u> (French)

ο and ω are both long "o" sounds.

υ after α, ε, η is a "v" sound. Thus,
   αυ = av (as in <u>av</u>ocado),
   ευ = ev (<u>ev</u>ery),
   ηυ = ay-v (as in "s<u>av</u>e")

Consonants

γ before ε, ει, ι = "y" sound as in "<u>y</u>et"
γ before other vowels = "gh" as in "<u>gh</u>ost"
δ = soft "th" or "dh" sound (**not** a hard "d" sound) as in "<u>th</u>e"

Consonant Pairs

γγ = "ng" sound (with the second gamma as in "get"); so, ἄγγελος = "an-ge-lohs"
γκ = "nk" sound as in "du<u>nk</u>"
γχ = "nkh sound as in "a<u>nkh</u>"
γξ = "nks" sound as in "tha<u>nks</u>"
ντ = "nd" sound; so -ονται is pronounced "own-deh"
μβ = "mv" sound as in "Hu<u>mv</u>ee"

ΚΑΤΑ ΙΩΑΝΝΗΝ

1:1 In the beginning was the Word, and the Word was with God, and the Word was God. 1:2 This one was in the beginning with God. 1:3 All things through him came into being, and without him not one thing came into being which has come into being. 1:4 In him was life, and the life was the light of people. 1:5 And the light keeps shining in the darkness, and *yet* the darkness did not understand it.

6 Ἐγένετο ἄνθρωπος ἀπεσταλμένος παρὰ θεοῦ, ὄνομα αὐτῷ Ἰωάννης· 7 οὗτος ἦλθεν εἰς μαρτυρίαν, ἵνα μαρτυρήσῃ περὶ τοῦ φωτός, ἵνα πάντες πιστεύσωσιν δι' αὐτοῦ. 8 οὐκ ἦν ἐκεῖνος τὸ φῶς, ἀλλ' ἵνα μαρτυρήσῃ περὶ τοῦ φωτός.

9 ἦν τὸ φῶς τὸ ἀληθινὸν ὃ φωτίζει πάντα ἄνθρωπον ἐρχόμενον εἰς τὸν κόσμον. 10 Ἐν τῷ κόσμῳ ἦν, καὶ ὁ κόσμος δι' αὐτοῦ ἐγένετο, καὶ ὁ κόσμος αὐτὸν οὐκ ἔγνω. 11 εἰς τὰ ἴδια ἦλθεν, καὶ οἱ ἴδιοι αὐτὸν οὐ παρέλαβον. 12 ὅσοι δὲ ἔλαβον αὐτόν, ἔδωκεν αὐτοῖς ἐξουσίαν τέκνα θεοῦ γενέσθαι, τοῖς πιστεύουσιν εἰς τὸ ὄνομα αὐτοῦ, 13 οἳ οὐκ ἐξ αἱμάτων οὐδὲ ἐκ θελήματος σαρκὸς οὐδὲ ἐκ θελήματος ἀνδρὸς ἀλλ' ἐκ θεοῦ ἐγεννήθησαν. 14 Καὶ ὁ λόγος σὰρξ ἐγένετο καὶ ἐσκήνωσεν ἐν ἡμῖν, καὶ ἐθεασάμεθα τὴν δόξαν αὐτοῦ, δόξαν ὡς μονογενοῦς παρὰ πατρός, πλήρης χάριτος καὶ ἀληθείας·

1:6 There came a person having been sent out from God, his name *was* John. 1:7 This one came as a testimony, in order that he would testify about the light, in order that all would believe through him. 1:8 That one (*John*) was not the light, but *he came* in order that he would testify about the light. 1:9 He (*the Word*) was the true light, which shines on every person, coming into the world. 1:10 He was in the world, and the world came into being through him, and *yet* the world did not know him. 1:11 He came to his own, and *yet* his own did not receive him. 1:12 But as many as received him, he gave to them authority to become children of God, to the ones that are believing in his name, 1:13 *the ones* who not from blood, nor from the will of the flesh, nor from the will of a man, but from God were born. 1:14 And the word became flesh and encamped among us, and we beheld his glory, glory as the only One from the Father, full of grace and truth.

1:15 (John continues testifying about him and he has cried out, saying, "This one was *the one* whom I spoke about, 'The one that is coming after me has existed before me, because he was first before me.') **1:16** Because from his fulfillment *in coming*, we ourselves, all of us, have also received grace in exchange for grace, **1:17** because the law was given through Moses, yet grace and truth came through Jesus Christ. **1:18** No one has seen God ever. The only God, the One that is in the bosom of the Father, that one described *him* in detail. **1:19** And this is John's testimony when the Jewish officials from Jerusalem sent priests and Levites, in order that they would ask him, "You, who are you?" **1:20** And he confessed and did not deny, yet he confessed this: "I myself am not the messiah." **1:21** And they asked him, "What then? You, are you Elijah?" And he says, "I am not." "Are you the prophet?" And he answered back, "No." **1:22** Therefore, they said to him, "Who are you? *Tell us* in order that we would give an answer to the ones that sent us: What do you *usually* say about yourself?" **1:23** He kept saying, "I *am* a voice of one shouting in the wilderness: 'Make straight the way of the Lord,' just as the prophet Isaiah spoke." **1:24** And they were sent out from the Pharisees, **1:25** and *so* they asked him and said to him, "Then, why are you baptizing if you yourself are neither the Christ, nor Elijah, nor the prophet?

1:26 John answered back to them saying, "I myself am baptizing in water; in your midst one has stood up, whom you yourselves do not know, 1:27 the one that is coming after me, of whom I am not worthy, that I untie the strap of his sandal. 1:28 These things happened in Bethany on the other side of the Jordan, where John was baptizing. 1:29 On the next day he sees Jesus coming toward him, and he begins saying, "Look, the Lamb of God, the one that is taking away the sin of the world. 1:30 This is he about whom I myself said, 'After me is coming a man, who has existed before me, because he was first before me. 1:31 And I myself did not know him, but in order that he would be made visible to Israel, for this reason, I myself came baptizing in water.'" 1:32 And John testified saying this: "I have beheld the Spirit coming down like a dove from heaven, and it remained upon him. 1:33 And I myself did not know him, but, the one that sent me to baptize in water, that one, he said to me, 'Upon whomever you see the Spirit descending and remaining on him, this one is the one that is baptizing in the Holy Spirit.' 1:34 And I myself have seen, and I have testified that, this one is the chosen one of God."

1:35 On the next day, once again John had stood up, and two of his disciples, 1:36 and after he looked at Jesus walking around, he began saying, "Look, the Lamb of God!" 1:37 And his two disciples heard him speaking and they followed Jesus. 1:38 But, Jesus, after turning and observing them following says to them, "What are you looking for?" And they said to him, "My Teacher (which, when spoken, is translated 'Teacher'), where are you staying?" 1:39 He says to them, "Come and you will see!" Therefore, they came and saw where he was staying, and they stayed with him that day. It was about the tenth hour. 1:40 Andrew was the brother of Simon Peter, one of the two that heard from John and followed him. 1:41 First, this one finds his own brother Simon and begins saying to him, "We have found the Messiah (which is translated 'Christ'). 1:42 He brought him to Jesus. After seeing him, Jesus said, "You are Simon, the son of John; you yourself will be called Cephas (which is translated 'Peter')." 1:43 On the next day he wanted to go out into the Galilee. And he finds Philip and Jesus begins saying to him, "Follow me!" 1:44 Moreover, Philip was from Bethsaida, from the city of Andrew and Peter.

1:45–2:1

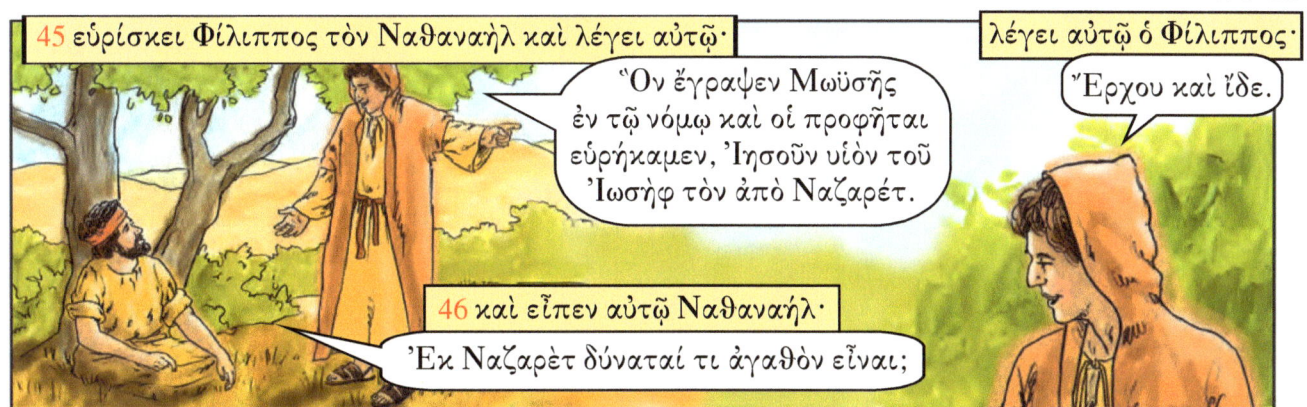

1:45 Philip finds Nathanial and begins saying to him, "*The one* whom Moses in the law wrote *about*, and the prophets, we have found, Jesus, the son of Joseph from Nazareth." **1:46** And Nathanial said to him, "Is it possible for anything good to be from Nazareth?" Philip keeps saying to him, "Come and see!" **1:47** Jesus saw Nathanial coming towards him and he begins saying about him, "See, truly *he is* an Israelite, in whom there is no deceit!" **1:48** Nathanial says to him, "From where do you know me?" Jesus answered back and said to him, "Before Philip called you, while being under the fig tree, I saw you." **1:49** Nathanial answered back to him, "My Teacher, you yourself are the Son of God! You yourself are the King of Israel!" **1:50** Jesus answered back and said to him, "Because I told to you that I saw you underneath the fig tree, you believe? Greater things than these you will see!" **1:51** And he says to him, "Amen! Amen! I am telling you, you will see the heaven opened up and the angels of God ascending and descending upon the Son of Man." **2:1** And on the third day a wedding occurred in Cana of the Galilee, and the mother of Jesus was there.

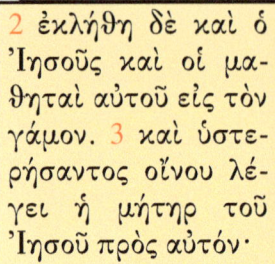

2:2 Moreover, Jesus was invited, and his disciples, to the wedding. 2:3 And when the wine was gone, the mother of Jesus says to him, "They have no wine." 2:4 And Jesus says to her, "What does that have to do with me and you, lady? My hour has not yet arrived." 2:5 His mother says to the servants, "Whatsoever he tells you, you do it!" 2:6 Now there were six stone water jars there according to the purification rites of the Jews set up, holding upwards of two or three measures. 2:7 Jesus says to them, "Fill the water jars with water!" And they filled them up to the top. 2:8 And he continues saying to them, "Now, draw *some* and take *it* to the head waiter." And they took *it*. 2:9 And when the head waiter tasted the water having become wine, even he did not know where it came from, but the servants that had drawn the water knew; *so* the head waiter calls for the groom, 2:10 and he says to him, "Every person sets out first the good wine, and, whenever they become drunk, *then* the lesser *wine*: you yourself have kept the good wine until now!" 2:11 Jesus did this initial one of the signs in Cana of the Galilee and manifested his glory, and his disciples believed in him.

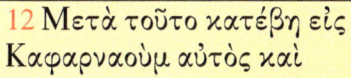
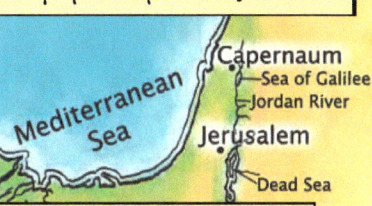

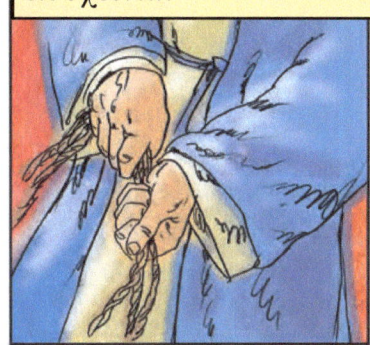

2:12 After this he went down to Capernaum, he and his mother and brothers and his disciples; and there they did not remain many days. 2:13 And the Passover of the Jews was near, and Jesus went up into Jerusalem. 2:14 And he found in the temple the ones that are selling oxen and sheep and doves and the moneychangers sitting; 2:15 and making a whip out of cords, he drove all out of the temple, both the sheep and the oxen, and he poured out the coins of the small coin exchangers and turned over the tables; 2:16 and to the ones that are selling the doves he said, "Take away these things from in here! Don't keep making the house of my father a house of merchandise!" 2:17 (His disciples remembered that it is written, "Zeal for your house will consume me.") 2:18 The Jewish officials, therefore, answered back and said to him, "What sign are you demonstrating against us, in that you are doing these things?" 2:19 Jesus answered back and said to them, "Destroy this temple and in three days I will raise it up!" 2:20 The Jewish officials, therefore, said, "In the span of forty six years this temple was built, and you yourself, in three days, will raise it up?!"

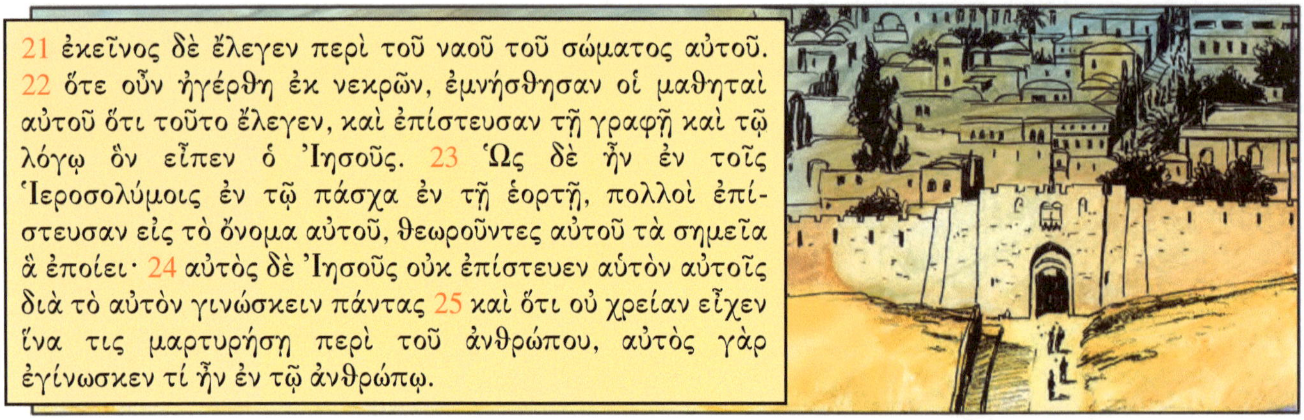

21 ἐκεῖνος δὲ ἔλεγεν περὶ τοῦ ναοῦ τοῦ σώματος αὐτοῦ. 22 ὅτε οὖν ἠγέρθη ἐκ νεκρῶν, ἐμνήσθησαν οἱ μαθηταὶ αὐτοῦ ὅτι τοῦτο ἔλεγεν, καὶ ἐπίστευσαν τῇ γραφῇ καὶ τῷ λόγῳ ὃν εἶπεν ὁ Ἰησοῦς. 23 Ὡς δὲ ἦν ἐν τοῖς Ἱεροσολύμοις ἐν τῷ πάσχα ἐν τῇ ἑορτῇ, πολλοὶ ἐπίστευσαν εἰς τὸ ὄνομα αὐτοῦ, θεωροῦντες αὐτοῦ τὰ σημεῖα ἃ ἐποίει· 24 αὐτὸς δὲ Ἰησοῦς οὐκ ἐπίστευεν αὑτὸν αὐτοῖς διὰ τὸ αὐτὸν γινώσκειν πάντας 25 καὶ ὅτι οὐ χρείαν εἶχεν ἵνα τις μαρτυρήσῃ περὶ τοῦ ἀνθρώπου, αὐτὸς γὰρ ἐγίνωσκεν τί ἦν ἐν τῷ ἀνθρώπῳ.

Chapter 3

3:1 Ἦν δὲ ἄνθρωπος ἐκ τῶν Φαρισαίων, Νικόδημος ὄνομα αὐτῷ, ἄρχων τῶν Ἰουδαίων· 2 οὗτος ἦλθεν πρὸς αὐτὸν νυκτὸς καὶ εἶπεν αὐτῷ·

Ῥαββί, οἴδαμεν ὅτι ἀπὸ θεοῦ ἐλήλυθας διδάσκαλος· οὐδεὶς γὰρ δύναται ταῦτα τὰ σημεῖα ποιεῖν ἃ σὺ ποιεῖς, ἐὰν μὴ ᾖ ὁ θεὸς μετ' αὐτοῦ.

3 ἀπεκρίθη Ἰησοῦς καὶ εἶπεν αὐτῷ·

Ἀμήν. Ἀμήν. Λέγω σοι, ἐὰν μή τις γεννηθῇ ἄνωθεν, οὐ δύναται ἰδεῖν τὴν βασιλείαν τοῦ θεοῦ.

4 λέγει πρὸς αὐτὸν ὁ Νικόδημος·

Πῶς δύναται ἄνθρωπος γεννηθῆναι γέρων ὤν; μὴ δύναται εἰς τὴν κοιλίαν τῆς μητρὸς αὐτοῦ δεύτερον εἰσελθεῖν καὶ γεννηθῆναι;

5 ἀπεκρίθη Ἰησοῦς·

Ἀμήν. Ἀμήν. Λέγω σοι, ἐὰν μή τις γεννηθῇ ἐξ ὕδατος καὶ πνεύματος, οὐ δύναται εἰσελθεῖν εἰς τὴν βασιλείαν τοῦ θεοῦ. 6 τὸ γεγεννημένον ἐκ τῆς σαρκὸς σάρξ ἐστιν, καὶ τὸ γεγεννημένον ἐκ τοῦ πνεύματος πνεῦμά ἐστιν. 7 μὴ θαυμάσῃς ὅτι εἶπόν σοι Δεῖ ὑμᾶς γεννηθῆναι ἄνωθεν. 8 τὸ πνεῦμα ὅπου θέλει πνεῖ, καὶ τὴν φωνὴν αὐτοῦ ἀκούεις, ἀλλ' οὐκ οἶδας πόθεν ἔρχεται καὶ ποῦ ὑπάγει· οὕτως ἐστὶν πᾶς ὁ γεγεννημένος ἐκ τοῦ πνεύματος.

2:21 Well, that one (*Jesus*) was speaking about the temple of his body. 2:22 When, therefore, he was raised from the dead, his disciples remembered that he would keep saying this, and they believed the Scripture and the word which Jesus spoke. 2:23 Additionally, when he was in Jerusalem at the Passover during the Feast, many trusted in his name, while observing his signs which he was doing. 2:24 But Jesus himself did not entrust himself to them, because he was knowing about *them* all, 2:25 and because he was having no need that someone testify about humanity, for he himself was knowing about what was in humanity. 3:1 Now there was a person from the Pharisees, Nicodemus *was* his name, a ruler of the Jews. 3:2 This man came to him by night and said to him, "My Master, we know that you, a teacher, have come from God; for no one is able to do these signs which you yourself are doing, unless God was with him." 3:3 Jesus answered back and said to him, "Amen! Amen! I say to you, unless someone is born from above, he is not able to see the kingdom of God." 3:4 Nicodemus says to him, "How is a person able to be born when being old? He's not able to enter into the womb of his mother a second time and be born, is he? (No!)" 3:5 Jesus answered back, "Amen! Amen! I keep saying to you, unless someone is born from water and Spirit, he is not able to enter into the Kingdom of God. 3:6 The one that has been born from the flesh is flesh, and the one that has been born from the Spirit is spirit. 3:7 Do not be amazed that I said to you, 'You must be born from above'! 3:8 The Spirit breathes where it wants, and you hear its voice, but you do not know from where it comes and where it goes; it is this way for everyone born of the Spirit."

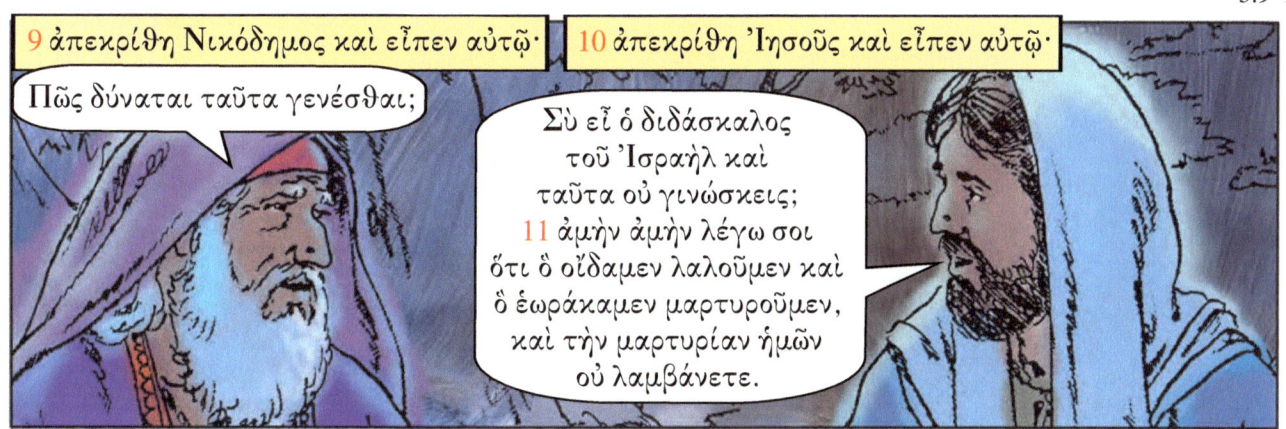

9 ἀπεκρίθη Νικόδημος καὶ εἶπεν αὐτῷ·

Πῶς δύναται ταῦτα γενέσθαι;

10 ἀπεκρίθη Ἰησοῦς καὶ εἶπεν αὐτῷ·

Σὺ εἶ ὁ διδάσκαλος τοῦ Ἰσραὴλ καὶ ταῦτα οὐ γινώσκεις; 11 ἀμὴν ἀμὴν λέγω σοι ὅτι ὃ οἴδαμεν λαλοῦμεν καὶ ὃ ἑωράκαμεν μαρτυροῦμεν, καὶ τὴν μαρτυρίαν ἡμῶν οὐ λαμβάνετε.

12 εἰ τὰ ἐπίγεια εἶπον ὑμῖν καὶ οὐ πιστεύετε, πῶς ἐὰν εἴπω ὑμῖν τὰ ἐπουράνια πιστεύσετε; 13 καὶ οὐδεὶς ἀναβέβηκεν εἰς τὸν οὐρανὸν εἰ μὴ ὁ ἐκ τοῦ οὐρανοῦ καταβάς, ὁ υἱὸς τοῦ ἀνθρώπου. 14 καὶ καθὼς Μωϋσῆς ὕψωσεν τὸν ὄφιν ἐν τῇ ἐρήμῳ, οὕτως ὑψωθῆναι δεῖ τὸν υἱὸν τοῦ ἀνθρώπου, 15 ἵνα πᾶς ὁ πιστεύων ἐν αὐτῷ ἔχῃ ζωὴν αἰώνιον. 16 Οὕτως γὰρ ἠγάπησεν ὁ θεὸς τὸν κόσμον ὥστε τὸν υἱὸν τὸν μονογενῆ ἔδωκεν, ἵνα πᾶς ὁ πιστεύων εἰς αὐτὸν μὴ ἀπόληται ἀλλὰ ἔχῃ ζωὴν αἰώνιον. 17 οὐ γὰρ ἀπέστειλεν ὁ θεὸς τὸν υἱὸν εἰς τὸν κόσμον ἵνα κρίνῃ τὸν κόσμον, ἀλλ' ἵνα σωθῇ ὁ κόσμος δι' αὐτοῦ. 18 ὁ πιστεύων εἰς αὐτὸν οὐ κρίνεται· ὁ δὲ μὴ πιστεύων ἤδη κέκριται, ὅτι μὴ πεπίστευκεν εἰς τὸ ὄνομα τοῦ μονογενοῦς υἱοῦ τοῦ θεοῦ. 19 αὕτη δέ ἐστιν ἡ κρίσις ὅτι τὸ φῶς ἐλήλυθεν εἰς τὸν κόσμον καὶ ἠγάπησαν οἱ ἄνθρωποι μᾶλλον τὸ σκότος ἢ τὸ φῶς, ἦν γὰρ αὐτῶν πονηρὰ τὰ ἔργα.

3:9 Nicodemus answered back and said to him, "How are these things able to happen?" 3:10 Jesus answered back and said to him, "Are you yourself the teacher of Israel and you do not know these things? 3:11 Amen! Amen! I keep telling you this: 'That which we know we continue speaking about and that which we have seen we continue testifying about, and you are not accepting our testimony. 3:12 If I spoke to you of earthly things and you continue not believing, how, if I speak to you of heavenly things, will you believe? 3:13 And no one has ascended into heaven, except the one that descended out of heaven, the Son of Humanity. 3:14 And just as Moses lifted the serpent up in the wilderness, in the same manner the Son of Humanity must be lifted up, 3:15 in order that every person believing in him would have everlasting life. 3:16 For in this manner God loved the world that he gave his one and only Son, in order that every person believing in him would not perish, but would have everlasting life. 3:17 For God did not send the Son into the world in order that he would judge the world, but in order that the world would be saved through him. 3:18 The one that is believing in him is not being judged; but the one that is not believing already has been judged, because he has not believed in the name of the one and only Son of God. 3:19 Moreover, this is the judgment, *namely* that the Light has come into the world and the people loved the darkness more than the Light, for their deeds were evil.

3:20 For everyone doing evil things keeps hating the Light and does not go toward the light, in order that his deeds would not be exposed. 3:21 But the one that is doing the truth continues going toward the Light, in order that his deeds would be manifest that they have been accomplished in God." 3:22 After these things, Jesus went, and his disciples, into the Judean land, and there he was spending time with them and he continued baptizing. 3:23 Well, John was also baptizing in Ainon near Saleim, because there was much water there, and they kept coming and kept being baptized. 3:24 For John was not yet cast into prison. 3:25 Therefore, a controversy took place from John's disciples with a Jewish man about purification. 3:26 And they came to John and said to him, "My Master, *the one* who was with you across the Jordan, to whom you yourself have testified, look, this one keeps baptizing and all of them are going to him!" 3:27 John answered back and said, "A person is not able to receive a single thing, unless it has been given to him out of heaven. 3:28 You yourselves are continually bearing witness to me that I said, 'I myself am not the Christ!' but I said this: 'I am being sent ahead of that one.'

29 ὁ ἔχων τὴν νύμφην νυμφίος ἐστίν· ὁ δὲ φίλος τοῦ νυμφίου ὁ ἑστηκὼς καὶ ἀκούων αὐτοῦ, χαρᾷ χαίρει διὰ τὴν φωνὴν τοῦ νυμφίου. αὕτη οὖν ἡ χαρὰ ἡ ἐμὴ πεπλήρωται. 30 ἐκεῖνον δεῖ αὐξάνειν, ἐμὲ δὲ ἐλαττοῦσθαι.

31 Ὁ ἄνωθεν ἐρχόμενος ἐπάνω πάντων ἐστίν. ὁ ὢν ἐκ τῆς γῆς ἐκ τῆς γῆς ἐστιν καὶ ἐκ τῆς γῆς λαλεῖ· ὁ ἐκ τοῦ οὐρανοῦ ἐρχόμενος ἐπάνω πάντων ἐστίν· 32 ὃ ἑώρακεν καὶ ἤκουσεν τοῦτο μαρτυρεῖ, καὶ τὴν μαρτυρίαν αὐτοῦ οὐδεὶς λαμβάνει. 33 ὁ λαβὼν αὐτοῦ τὴν μαρτυρίαν ἐσφράγισεν ὅτι ὁ θεὸς ἀληθής ἐστιν.

34 ὃν γὰρ ἀπέστειλεν ὁ θεὸς τὰ ῥήματα τοῦ θεοῦ λαλεῖ, οὐ γὰρ ἐκ μέτρου δίδωσιν τὸ πνεῦμα. 35 ὁ πατὴρ ἀγαπᾷ τὸν υἱόν, καὶ πάντα δέδωκεν ἐν τῇ χειρὶ αὐτοῦ. 36 ὁ πιστεύων εἰς τὸν υἱὸν ἔχει ζωὴν αἰώνιον· ὁ δὲ ἀπειθῶν τῷ υἱῷ οὐκ ὄψεται ζωήν, ἀλλ' ἡ ὀργὴ τοῦ θεοῦ μένει ἐπ' αὐτόν.

Chapter 4

4:1 Ὡς οὖν ἔγνω ὁ Ἰησοῦς ὅτι ἤκουσαν οἱ Φαρισαῖοι ὅτι Ἰησοῦς πλείονας μαθητὰς ποιεῖ καὶ βαπτίζει ἢ Ἰωάννης—2 καίτοιγε Ἰησοῦς αὐτὸς οὐκ ἐβάπτιζεν ἀλλ' οἱ μαθηταὶ αὐτοῦ—3 ἀφῆκεν τὴν Ἰουδαίαν καὶ ἀπῆλθεν πάλιν εἰς τὴν Γαλιλαίαν. 4 ἔδει δὲ αὐτὸν διέρχεσθαι διὰ τῆς Σαμαρείας. 5 ἔρχεται οὖν εἰς πόλιν τῆς Σαμαρείας λεγομένην Συχὰρ πλησίον τοῦ χωρίου ὃ ἔδωκεν Ἰακὼβ τῷ Ἰωσὴφ τῷ υἱῷ αὐτοῦ·

3:29 The one that is having the bride is the groom; but the friend of the groom standing and hearing him rejoices with joy because of the voice of the groom. Therefore, this joy of mine has been fulfilled! 3:30 That man must increase, but I myself must decrease. 3:31 The one that is coming from above is above all people. The one that is from the earth is from the earth and he keeps speaking *in a manner* from the earth; the one that is coming from heaven is above all people. 3:32 That which he has seen and heard, this he continues testifying, and his testimony no one is receiving 3:33 The one that receives his testimony guarantees that God is true. 3:34 For he whom God sent continues speaking the words of God, for without measure he is giving the Spirit. 3:35 The Father loves the Son, and all things he has given into his hand. 3:36 The one that is believing in the Son continues having everlasting life; but the one that is disobeying the Son will not see life, but the wrath of God keeps remaining upon him. 4:1 Therefore, when Jesus knew that the Pharisees heard this: "Jesus makes and baptizes more disciples than John" 4:2 (although Jesus himself was not baptizing but rather his disciples *were*), 4:3 he left Judea and departed again into The Galilee. 4:4 Now, he was needing to go through Samaria. 4:5 Therefore, he comes into a city of Samaria called Sychar near the area which Jacob gave to Joseph his son.

4:6 Moreover, Jacob's well was there. Jesus, therefore, being tired from his journey, was sitting in this manner upon the well; it was about the sixth hour. 4:7 A woman from Samaria comes to draw water. Jesus says to her, "Give me *water* to drink!" 4:8 For his disciples had gone away into the city, in order that they would buy food. 4:9 Therefore, the Samaritan woman says to him, "How are you, being a Jew, asking to drink *water* from me being a Samaritan woman? For Jews do not associate with Samaritans." 4:10 Jesus answered back and said to her, "If you had known the gift of God and who is the one that is speaking to you, 'Give me *water* to drink!', then you yourself would have asked him and he would have given you living water." 4:11 The woman continues speaking to him, "Sir, you do not even have a bucket and the well is deep; so, where are you holding this living water? 4:12 Surely you yourself are not greater than our father, Jacob, who gave us the well and himself drank from out of it, and his sons, and his cattle, are you? (No!)" 4:13 Jesus answered back and said to her, "Everyone drinking from this water will thirst again; 4:14 but, whoever shall drink of the water which I will give him, he will never thirst in this age; but the water which I will give him will become in him a spring of water springing up into everlasting life." 4:15 The woman continues saying to him, "Sir, give me this water, in order that I would neither be thirsty nor continue coming here to draw *water*!" 4:16 He continues saying to her, "Go, call your husband and come here!" 4:17 The woman answered back and said to him, "I don't have a husband." Jesus continues speaking to her, "You spoke this well: 'I have no husband.'

Jesus continues speaking to her, "You spoke this well: 'I have no husband.' 4:18 For you had five husbands, and now *the one* whom you have is not your husband; you have spoken about this matter truly." 4:19 The woman continues saying to him, "Sir, I perceive that you yourself are a prophet. 4:20 Our fathers worshiped in this mountain; and you yourselves continue saying this: 'In Jerusalem is the place where one must worship.'" 4:21 Jesus continues saying to her, "Believe me, woman, that the hour is coming when neither in this mountain nor in Jerusalem will you *people* worship the Father. 4:22 You yourselves keep worshiping that which you do not know, we ourselves worship that which we know, because salvation is from the Jews. 4:23 But the hour is coming and now is, when the true worshipers will worship the Father in spirit and truth; for indeed the Father continues seeking such ones as these worshiping him. 4:24 God is Spirit, and the ones that are worshiping him must worship in spirit and truth." 4:25 The woman continues saying to him, "I know that a Messiah is coming, the One that is called Christ; whenever that man comes, he will announce to us all things." 4:26 Jesus says to her, "I am he, the one speaking to you."

4:27 And at this point his disciples came, and they were expressing amazement that he was speaking with a woman; yet, no one said, "What are you seeking?" or "Why are you speaking with her?" 4:28 Therefore, the woman left her water jar and went away into the city and she begins speaking to the people, 4:29 "Come, see a person who spoke to me all things, how much I did! This man isn't the Christ, is he? (No, *he couldn't be!*)" 4:30 They went out of the city and were going to him. 4:31 In the meantime, the disciples kept begging him, saying, "Rabbi, eat!" 4:32 But he said to them, "I myself have food to eat which you yourselves don't know about." 4:33 Therefore, the disciples kept saying to one another, "Someone didn't bring him *something* to eat, did he? (No.) 4:34 Jesus continues speaking to them, "My food is that I do the will of the one that sent me and I will complete this work of his. 4:35 Don't you yourselves say this: 'There are still four months and the harvest is coming'? (Yes *you do!*) Look, I am telling you, 'Lift up your eyes and look at the fields, because they are white for harvest. 4:36 Already the one that is reaping receives a wage and gathers fruit for everlasting life, in order that the one that is sowing would rejoice together also *with* the one that is reaping. 4:37 For in this way, the saying is true that one is the one that is sowing and another is the one that is reaping. 4:38 I myself sent you to reap *that* for which you yourselves have not labored: others have labored, and you yourselves have entered into their labor."

16

39 Ἐκ δὲ τῆς πόλεως ἐκείνης πολλοὶ ἐπίστευσαν εἰς αὐτὸν τῶν Σαμαριτῶν διὰ τὸν λόγον τῆς γυναικὸς μαρτυρούσης ὅτι Εἶπέν μοι πάντα ἃ ἐποίησα. 40 ὡς οὖν ἦλθον πρὸς αὐτὸν οἱ Σαμαρῖται, ἠρώτων αὐτὸν μεῖναι παρ' αὐτοῖς· καὶ ἔμεινεν ἐκεῖ δύο ἡμέρας. 41 καὶ πολλῷ πλείους ἐπίστευσαν διὰ τὸν λόγον αὐτοῦ, 42 τῇ τε γυναικὶ ἔλεγον ὅτι

Οὐκέτι διὰ τὴν σὴν λαλιὰν πιστεύομεν· αὐτοὶ γὰρ ἀκηκόαμεν, καὶ οἴδαμεν ὅτι οὗτός ἐστιν ἀληθῶς ὁ σωτὴρ τοῦ κόσμου.

43 Μετὰ δὲ τὰς δύο ἡμέρας ἐξῆλθεν ἐκεῖθεν εἰς τὴν Γαλιλαίαν· 44 αὐτὸς γὰρ Ἰησοῦς ἐμαρτύρησεν ὅτι προφήτης ἐν τῇ ἰδίᾳ πατρίδι τιμὴν οὐκ ἔχει. 45 ὅτε οὖν ἦλθεν εἰς τὴν Γαλιλαίαν, ἐδέξαντο αὐτὸν οἱ Γαλιλαῖοι, πάντα ἑωρακότες ὅσα ἐποίησεν ἐν Ἱεροσολύμοις ἐν τῇ ἑορτῇ, καὶ αὐτοὶ γὰρ ἦλθον εἰς τὴν ἑορτήν. 46 Ἦλθεν οὖν πάλιν εἰς τὴν Κανὰ τῆς Γαλιλαίας, ὅπου ἐποίησεν τὸ ὕδωρ οἶνον. καὶ ἦν τις βασιλικὸς οὗ ὁ υἱὸς ἠσθένει ἐν Καφαρναούμ.

4:39 Well, from that city many of the Samaritans believed in him because of the word of the woman testifying this: "He told me all the things which I did." 4:40 Therefore, as the Samaritans came to him, they kept asking him to remain with them; and he remained there two days. 4:41 And to a greater degree more *of them* believed because of his word, 4:42 and to the woman they kept saying this: "No longer are we believing *only* because of your speech; for we ourselves have heard, and we know that this one is truly the Savior of the world." 4:43 Well, after two days he went out from there into The Galilee. 4:44 For Jesus himself testified that a prophet has no honor in his own hometown. 4:45 Therefore, when he came into The Galilee, the Galileans received him, having seen all things, how much he did in Jerusalem at the Feast *(of Passover)*, for they themselves also went for the Feast. 4:46 Therefore, he came again into Cana of The Galilee, where he made the water wine. And there was a certain ruler whose son was remaining sick in Capernaum.

4:47–5:1

4:47 This man, hearing that Jesus was arriving from Judaea into The Galilee, departed to him and kept asking that he would come down and heal his son, for he was about to die. 4:48 Therefore, Jesus said to him, "Unless you *all* see signs and wonders, you *all* will never ever believe." 4:49 The ruler continues saying to him, "Sir, come down before my child dies!" 4:50 Jesus says to him, "Go! Your son lives!" The person believed the word, which Jesus spoke to him, and he began going. 4:51 Well, already while he was going down, his servants met him saying that his son was living. 4:52 Therefore, he asked from them about the hour in which he became better. So, they told him this: "Yesterday at the seventh hour the fever left him." 4:53 Hence, the father knew that *it happened* at that hour in which Jesus said to him, "Your son lives," and he himself believed, and his whole house. 4:54 So, again Jesus performed this second sign after coming from Judaea into The Galilee. 5:1 After these things there was a feast of the Jews, and Jesus went up into Jerusalem.

18

5:2 Now there is in Jerusalem by the Sheep *Gate* a pool, the one that is called in Hebrew, Vaythesthah, having five porches. 5:3 On these were lying a multitude of ones being sick, blind, lame, withered away. 5:5 Well, a certain person was there, for thirty eight years being in his sickness. 5:6 Jesus, seeing this man lying down and knowing that he was already there a long time, begins saying to him: "Do you want to become well?" 5:7 The one that was being sick answered back to him, "Sir, I have nobody for the purpose that, when the water is stirred, he would throw me into the pool; but, while I am coming, another *person* goes down before me." 5:8 Jesus continues saying to him, "Start getting up, pick up your mat, and begin walking."

5:9 And straightway the person was made well and he picked up his mat and began walking. Well it was the Sabbath on that day. 5:10 Therefore, the Jewish Officials kept saying to the one that had been cured, "It is the Sabbath, and it is not lawful for you to pick up your bed. 5:11 But he answered back to them, "The one that made me well, that one said to me, "Pick up your mat and begin walking." 5:12 Therefore, they asked him, "Who is the person that said to you, 'Pick up and begin walking'?" 5:13 But the one that was healed did not know who he was, for Jesus turned away from the crowd that was in the place. 5:14 After these things Jesus finds him in the temple and said to him, "Look, you have been made well: continue sinning no longer, in order that something worse would not happen to you." 5:15 The person departed and announced to the Jewish Officials that Jesus was the one that made him well. 5:16 And because of this the Jewish Officials began persecuting Jesus, because he was doing these things on the Sabbath. 5:17 Well, Jesus answered back to them, "My Father until now is continually working and I am continually working." 5:18 Because of this, then, even more they kept seeking to kill him, because not only was he breaking the Sabbath, but also he kept saying his own father was God, thus making himself equal to God.

5:19 Therefore, Jesus answered back and kept saying to them, "Amen! Amen! I say to you, the Son is unable to do not one thing by himself unless he sees the Father doing something: for what ever things he does, these things also the Son does likewise. 5:20 For the Father loves the Son and shows him that which he himself is doing, and greater works than these he will show him, in order that you yourselves would be marveling. 5:21 For just as the Father is raising the dead and giving life, so also the Son is giving life to whom he is desiring. 5:22 For additionally the Father is not judging anyone, but all judgment he has given to the Son, 5:23 in order that all of them would honor the Son, just as they would honor the Father. The one that is not honoring the Son is not honoring the Father that sent him. 5:24 Amen! Amen! I am saying to you this: 'The one that is hearing my word and believing the one that sent me has everlasting life and is not entering into judgment, but has been transferred from death into life.' 5:25 Amen! Amen! I am saying to you this: 'The hour is coming and now is when the dead will hear the voice of the Son of God and the ones that heard will live. 5:26 For just as the Father has life in himself, so also he gave life to the Son to have in himself; 5:27 and he gave authority to him to execute judgment, because he is the Son of Humanity. 5:28 Do not be marveling at this, because the hour is coming in which all the ones in the tombs will hear his voice 5:29 and they will come out, the ones that did good deeds *will enter* into the resurrection of life, but the ones that committed bad deeds *will enter* into the resurrection of judgment.

30 Οὐ δύναμαι ἐγὼ ποιεῖν ἀπ' ἐμαυτοῦ οὐδέν· καθὼς ἀκούω κρίνω, καὶ ἡ κρίσις ἡ ἐμὴ δικαία ἐστίν, ὅτι οὐ ζητῶ τὸ θέλημα τὸ ἐμὸν ἀλλὰ τὸ θέλημα τοῦ πέμψαντός με. 31 Ἐὰν ἐγὼ μαρτυρῶ περὶ ἐμαυτοῦ, ἡ μαρτυρία μου οὐκ ἔστιν ἀληθής· 32 ἄλλος ἐστὶν ὁ μαρτυρῶν περὶ ἐμοῦ, καὶ οἶδα ὅτι ἀληθής ἐστιν ἡ μαρτυρία ἣν μαρτυρεῖ περὶ ἐμοῦ. 33 ὑμεῖς ἀπεστάλκατε πρὸς Ἰωάννην, καὶ μεμαρτύρηκε τῇ ἀληθείᾳ· 34 ἐγὼ δὲ οὐ παρὰ ἀνθρώπου τὴν μαρτυρίαν λαμβάνω, ἀλλὰ ταῦτα λέγω ἵνα ὑμεῖς σωθῆτε. 35 ἐκεῖνος ἦν ὁ λύχνος ὁ καιόμενος καὶ φαίνων, ὑμεῖς δὲ ἠθελήσατε ἀγαλλιαθῆναι πρὸς ὥραν ἐν τῷ φωτὶ αὐτοῦ·

36 ἐγὼ δὲ ἔχω τὴν μαρτυρίαν μείζω τοῦ Ἰωάννου, τὰ γὰρ ἔργα ἃ δέδωκέν μοι ὁ πατὴρ ἵνα τελειώσω αὐτά, αὐτὰ τὰ ἔργα ἃ ποιῶ, μαρτυρεῖ περὶ ἐμοῦ ὅτι ὁ πατήρ με ἀπέσταλκεν, 37 καὶ ὁ πέμψας με πατὴρ ἐκεῖνος μεμαρτύρηκεν περὶ ἐμοῦ. οὔτε φωνὴν αὐτοῦ πώποτε ἀκηκόατε οὔτε εἶδος αὐτοῦ ἑωράκατε, 38 καὶ τὸν λόγον αὐτοῦ οὐκ ἔχετε ἐν ὑμῖν μένοντα, ὅτι ὃν ἀπέστειλεν ἐκεῖνος τούτῳ ὑμεῖς οὐ πιστεύετε. 39 Ἐραυνᾶτε τὰς γραφάς, ὅτι ὑμεῖς δοκεῖτε ἐν αὐταῖς ζωὴν αἰώνιον ἔχειν· καὶ ἐκεῖναί εἰσιν αἱ μαρτυροῦσαι περὶ ἐμοῦ· 40 καὶ οὐ θέλετε ἐλθεῖν πρός με ἵνα ζωὴν ἔχητε. 41 δόξαν παρὰ ἀνθρώπων οὐ λαμβάνω, 42 ἀλλὰ ἔγνωκα ὑμᾶς ὅτι τὴν ἀγάπην τοῦ θεοῦ οὐκ ἔχετε ἐν ἑαυτοῖς. 43 ἐγὼ ἐλήλυθα ἐν τῷ ὀνόματι τοῦ πατρός μου καὶ οὐ λαμβάνετέ με· ἐὰν ἄλλος ἔλθῃ ἐν τῷ ὀνόματι τῷ ἰδίῳ, ἐκεῖνον λήμψεσθε. 44 πῶς δύνασθε ὑμεῖς πιστεῦσαι, δόξαν παρ' ἀλλήλων λαμβάνοντες, καὶ τὴν δόξαν τὴν παρὰ τοῦ μόνου θεοῦ οὐ ζητεῖτε; 45 μὴ δοκεῖτε ὅτι ἐγὼ κατηγορήσω ὑμῶν πρὸς τὸν πατέρα· ἔστιν ὁ κατηγορῶν ὑμῶν Μωϋσῆς, εἰς ὃν ὑμεῖς ἠλπίκατε. 46 εἰ γὰρ ἐπιστεύετε Μωϋσεῖ, ἐπιστεύετε ἂν ἐμοί, περὶ γὰρ ἐμοῦ ἐκεῖνος ἔγραψεν. 47 εἰ δὲ τοῖς ἐκείνου γράμμασιν οὐ πιστεύετε, πῶς τοῖς ἐμοῖς ῥήμασιν πιστεύσετε;

5:30 I am unable to do nothing by myself: just as I am hearing, I am judging, and my judgment is just, because I am not seeking my own will but the will of the one that sent me. 5:31 If I myself bear witness about myself, my testimony is not true. 5:32 Another is the one that is testifying about me, and I know that the testimony which he continues testifying about me is true. 5:33 You yourselves have sent *people* to John, and he has testified to the truth. 5:34 Well, I myself am not receiving testimony from a person, but I continue saying these things in order that you yourselves would be saved. 5:35 That one was the lamp that is burning and shining; moreover, you yourselves were willing to rejoice for an hour in his light. 5:36 But I myself have the testimony greater than John's, for the works, which the Father has given to me that I complete them, these very works, which I am doing, are testifying about me that the Father has sent me.

Chapter 6

6:1 Μετὰ ταῦτα ἀπῆλθεν ὁ Ἰησοῦς πέραν τῆς θαλάσσης τῆς Γαλιλαίας τῆς Τιβεριάδος. 2 ἠκολούθει δὲ αὐτῷ ὄχλος πολύς, ὅτι ἐθεώρουν τὰ σημεῖα ἃ ἐποίει ἐπὶ τῶν ἀσθενούντων.

5:37 And the one that sent me, the Father, has testified about me. Neither have you ever heard his voice nor have you seen his appearance. 5:38 And you are not having his word remaining in you, because the one whom that one sent, this one you yourselves continue not believing. 5:39 You keep searching the Scriptures, because you yourselves are supposing that in them you are having everlasting life; and these *Scriptures* are the ones that are testifying about me; 5:40 and you continue not wanting to come to me in order that you would have life. 5:41 I am not receiving glory from *mere* people, 5:42 but I know you, that you are not having the love of God in yourselves. 5:43 I myself have come in my Father's name and you continually do not receive me; if another person comes in his own name, you will receive him. 5:44 How are you yourselves able to believe while receiving glory from one another, and the glory that comes from the only God you continue not seeking? 5:45 You are not supposing that I myself will accuse you before the Father, are you? (No!) The one that is accusing you is Moses, into whom you yourself have set your hope. 5:46 For if you were believing Moses, you would be believing me; for that one wrote about me. 5:47 But if you continue not believing in the writings of that one, how will you believe my words?" 6:1 After these things Jesus went away to the other side of the Sea of Galilee of Tiberias. 6:2 Well, a large crowd began following him, because they were observing the signs which he was performing on the sick ones.

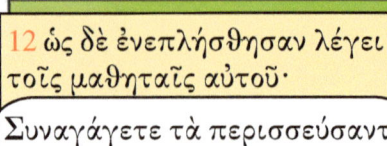
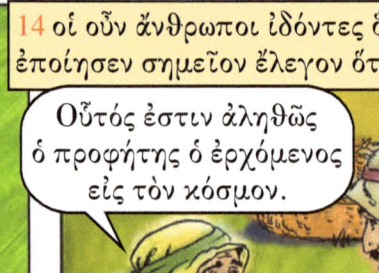

6:12 Well, as they were filled, he begins saying to his disciples, "Gather up the leftover pieces, in order that nothing would be lost." 6:13 Therefore, they gathered *them* up, and they filled twelve baskets with pieces from the five loaves, which were leftover by the ones who had eaten. 6:14 Therefore, the people, when seeing the sign which he did, kept saying this: "This one truly is the prophet coming into the world!" 6:15 Therefore, Jesus, realizing that they were about to come and seize him by force, in order that they would make him king, departed again into the mountain alone *by* himself. 6:16 Well, when evening came, his disciples went down onto the sea, 6:17 and, after embarking into a boat, they began going across the sea into Capernaum. And it had already become dark and Jesus had not yet come to them. 6:18 Additionally, the sea kept rising up, because a great wind was blowing.

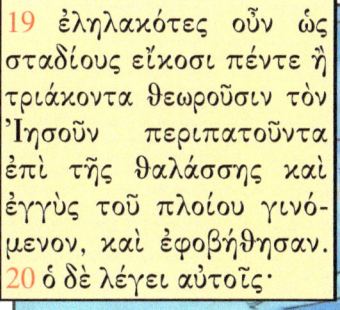

6:29 Jesus answered back and said to them, "This is the work of God, that you keep believing in that one whom he sent." 6:30 Therefore, they said to him, "So then, what sign are you yourself doing that we would see and believe you? What *works* are you working? 6:31 Our fathers ate the manna in the wilderness, just as it is written, 'Bread out of heaven he gave to them.'" 6:32 Therefore, Jesus said to them, "Amen! Amen! I am saying to you, Moses has not given to you the bread from heaven, but my Father is giving to you the bread from heaven *that is* true. 6:33 For the bread of God is the one coming down out of heaven and giving life to the world." 6:34 Therefore, they said to him, "Lord, always give this bread to us." 6:35 Jesus said to them: "I myself am the bread of life; the one coming to me will never hunger, and the one believing in me will never thirst ever. 6:36 But I told you this: indeed, you have seen me and you continue not believing. 6:37 Everyone, which the Father is giving to me, will come to me, and the one coming to me I will never cast out to the outside, 6:38 because I have come down from heaven, not in order that I would be doing my own will but the will of the one sending me; 6:39 Moreover, this is the will of the one sending me, that everyone, whom he has given to me, I would not lose from him, but I will raise him on the last day. 6:40 For this is the will of my Father: that everyone that beholds the Son and believes in him would have everlasting life, and I will raise him up on the last day."

6:41 Therefore, the Jewish oficial began murmuring about him because he said: "I myself am the bread coming down out of heaven." 6:42 And they kept saying, "Is this not Jesus, the son of Joseph, whose father and mother we know? (Yes!) How now does he keep saying this: 'I have come down out of heaven'?" 6:43 Jesus answered back and said to them, "Don't be complaining with one another. 6:44 No one is able to come to me unless the Father that sent me draws him, and I myself will raise him up on the last day. 6:45 It is written in the prophets, 'And all of them will be taught by God.' Everyone that hears from the Father and learns comes to me. 6:46 *It is* not that anyone has seen the Father, except the one that is from God, this one has seen the Father. 6:47 Amen! Amen! I am saying to you, the one that is believing has everlasting life. 6:48 I myself am the bread of life. 6:49 Your fathers ate the manna in the wilderness and they died. 6:50 This is the bread that is coming down out of heaven, in order that anyone would eat from it and not die. 6:51 I myself am the living bread that came down out of heaven: if anyone eats from this bread, he will live forever, and moreover the bread, which I myself will give, is my flesh on behalf of the life of the world." 6:52 Therefore, the Jewish officials began fighting with one another, saying, "How is this man able to give us his flesh to eat?"

6:53 Therefore, Jesus said to them, "Amen! Amen! I am saying to you, 'Unless you eat the flesh of the Son of Humanity and drink his blood, you are not having life within yourselves." 6:54 The one that is eating my flesh and drinking my blood continues having everlasting life: and I myself will raise him up at the last day. 6:55 For my flesh is true food, and my blood is true drink. 6:56 The one that is eating my flesh and drinking my blood continues remaining in me, and I in him. 6:57 Just as the living Father sent me, I myself also live on account of the Father, and the one that is eating me, that one also will live on account of me. 6:58 This is the bread that came down out of heaven, not just as the fathers ate and died; the one that is eating this bread will live in the age." 6:59 These things he said in a synagogue, teaching in Capernaum. 6:60 Therefore, many of his disciples, after hearing, said, "This is a hard saying; who is able to listen to it?" 6:61 But Jesus, knowing in himself that his disciples kept complaining about this, said to them, "Is this causing you to stumble?" 6:62 So *what* then if you behold the Son of Humanity ascending where he was before?! 6:63 The Spirit is the one giving life; the flesh benefits not one thing. The words which I myself have spoken to you are spirit and are life. 6:64 But there are some of you who are not believing." (For Jesus knew from the beginning who were the ones not believing and who was the one that would betray him.) 6:65 And he continued saying, "On account of this, I have said to you this: 'No one is able to come to me, unless it should be given to him from the Father.'"

6:66 From this *word*, many from his disciples departed in a backward manner, and no longer continued walking with him. 6:67 Therefore, Jesus said to the twelve, "You yourselves are not also wanting to go away, are you? *(No!)*" 6:68 Simon Peter answered back to him, "Lord, to whom would we depart? You have the words of everlasting life. 6:69 And we ourselves have believed and have known that you yourself are the Holy One of God." 6:70 Jesus answered back to them, "Did not I myself choose you the twelve? (Yes!) And from you one is an adversary!" 6:71 Moreover, he was speaking with regard to Judas the son of Simon Iscariot; for this one, one of the twelve, was about to hand him over. 7:1 And after these things Jesus began walking around in The Galilee. For he was not wanting to be walking around in Judaea, because the Jewish Officials kept seeking to kill him. 7:2 Now the Feast of the Jews, the Feast of Tabernacles, was near. 7:3 Therefore, his brothers said to him, "Leave from here and go into Judaea, in order that your disciples also would observe your works which you are doing. 7:4 For no one does something in secret and he himself seeks to be in public; if you are doing these things, show yourself to the world!" 7:5 For additionally, neither were his brothers believing in him. 7:6 Therefore, Jesus says to them, "My time is not yet present; but your time is always at hand. 7:7 The world is not able to continue hating you; but me, it keeps hating because I myself am testifying about it that its works are evil.

7:8 You yourselves go up to the feast; I myself am not going up to this feast, because my time has not yet been fulfilled." 7:9 So, after having said these things, he himself remained in The Galilee. 7:10 But, as his brothers went up to the feast, then also he himself went up, not in a showy manner, but as in secret. 7:11 Therefore, the Jewish Officials were seeking him at the feast and kept saying, "Where is that one?" 7:12 And there was much murmuring about him among the crowds. Some were saying this: "He is good!" But others were saying, "No, instead he is deceiving the crowd!" 7:13 However, no one was speaking publicly about him for fear of the Jewish Officials. 7:14 Now, while already The Feast was half over, Jesus went up into the temple and began teaching. 7:15 Therefore, the Jewish Officials kept being amazed saying, "How does this one know letters, since he has not learned *them*?" 7:16 Therefore, Jesus answered back to them and said, "My teaching is not mine, but belongs to the one that sent me.

7:17 If anyone wants to keep doing his will, he will know about the teaching, whether it is from God or *whether* I *indeed* am speaking from myself. 7:18 The one that is speaking from himself seeks his own glory; but the one that is seeking the glory of him that sent him, this one is true and there is no unrighteousness in him. 7:19 Has Moses not given you the law? (Yes!) And no one from you does the law. Why are you seeking to kill me?" 7:20 The crowd answered back, "You have a demon! Who is seeking to kill you?" 7:21 Jesus answered back and said to them, "I did one work and all of you are marveling. 7:22 Because of this, Moses has given you circumcision—not that it is from Moses, but from the fathers—and on the Sabbath you circumcise a person. 7:23 If a person receives circumcision on the Sabbath in order that the law of Moses would not be broken, are you mad at me because I made a whole person healthy on the Sabbath?! 7:24 Don't keep judging according to sight, but begin making the righteous judgment!"

7:25–34

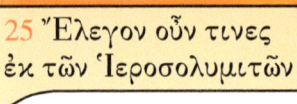
25 Ἔλεγον οὖν τινες ἐκ τῶν Ἱεροσολυμιτῶν·

Οὐχ οὗτός ἐστιν ὃν ζητοῦσιν ἀποκτεῖναι; 26 καὶ ἴδε παρρησίᾳ λαλεῖ καὶ οὐδὲν αὐτῷ λέγουσιν· μήποτε ἀληθῶς ἔγνωσαν οἱ ἄρχοντες ὅτι οὗτός ἐστιν ὁ χριστός;

27 ἀλλὰ τοῦτον οἴδαμεν πόθεν ἐστίν· ὁ δὲ χριστὸς ὅταν ἔρχηται οὐδεὶς γινώσκει πόθεν ἐστίν.

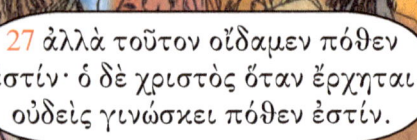
28 ἔκραξεν οὖν ἐν τῷ ἱερῷ διδάσκων ὁ Ἰησοῦς καὶ λέγων·

Κἀμὲ οἴδατε καὶ οἴδατε πόθεν εἰμί· καὶ ἀπ' ἐμαυτοῦ οὐκ ἐλήλυθα, ἀλλ' ἔστιν ἀληθινὸς ὁ πέμψας με, ὃν ὑμεῖς οὐκ οἴδατε· 29 ἐγὼ οἶδα αὐτόν, ὅτι παρ' αὐτοῦ εἰμι κἀκεῖνός με ἀπέστειλεν.

30 ἐζήτουν οὖν αὐτὸν πιάσαι, καὶ οὐδεὶς ἐπέβαλεν ἐπ' αὐτὸν τὴν χεῖρα, ὅτι οὔπω ἐληλύθει ἡ ὥρα αὐτοῦ. 31 ἐκ τοῦ ὄχλου δὲ πολλοὶ ἐπίστευσαν εἰς αὐτόν, καὶ ἔλεγον·

Ὁ χριστὸς ὅταν ἔλθῃ μὴ πλείονα σημεῖα ποιήσει ὧν οὗτος ἐποίησεν;

32 Ἤκουσαν οἱ Φαρισαῖοι τοῦ ὄχλου γογγύζοντος περὶ αὐτοῦ ταῦτα, καὶ ἀπέστειλαν οἱ ἀρχιερεῖς καὶ οἱ Φαρισαῖοι ὑπηρέτας ἵνα πιάσωσιν αὐτόν. 33 εἶπεν οὖν ὁ Ἰησοῦς·

Ἔτι χρόνον μικρὸν μεθ' ὑμῶν εἰμι καὶ ὑπάγω πρὸς τὸν πέμψαντά με. 34 ζητήσετέ με καὶ οὐχ εὑρήσετε, καὶ ὅπου εἰμὶ ἐγὼ ὑμεῖς οὐ δύνασθε ἐλθεῖν.

7:25 Therefore, some of them from the Jerusalemites began saying, "Isn't this him whom they were seeking to kill? 7:26 And look, he is speaking publicly and they are say nothing against him. It isn't somehow that truly the rulers knew that this one is the Anointed One, is it? (No!) 7:27 However, we know this man, where he is from: but the Anointed One, whenever he comes, no one knows where he is from. 7:28 Therefore, Jesus shouted in the temple, teaching and saying, "Both you know me and know where I am from; and I have not come from myself, but the one that sent me is true, whom you yourselves do not know. 7:29 I myself know him, because I am from beside him, and that one sent me. 7:30 Therefore, they began seeking to seize him: and no one laid a hand on him, because his hour had not yet come. 7:31 Moreover, many from the crowd trusted in him, and they kept saying, "The Anointed One, whenever he comes, he will not do more signs than this one did, will he? (No!) 7:32 The Pharisees heard the multitude murmuring these things concerning him; and the chief priests and the Pharisees sent officers in order that they would seize him. 7:33 Therefore Jesus said, "Still a little while am I with you, and I am going to the one that sent me. 7:34 You will seek me and will not find, and where I myself am, you yourself are not able to come.

7:35–44

35 εἶπον οὖν οἱ Ἰουδαῖοι πρὸς ἑαυτούς·

Ποῦ οὗτος μέλλει πορεύεσθαι ὅτι ἡμεῖς οὐχ εὑρήσομεν αὐτόν; μὴ εἰς τὴν διασπορὰν τῶν Ἑλλήνων μέλλει πορεύεσθαι καὶ διδάσκειν τοὺς Ἕλληνας;

36 τίς ἐστιν ὁ λόγος οὗτος ὃν εἶπε· Ζητήσετέ με καὶ οὐχ εὑρήσετε, καὶ ὅπου εἰμὶ ἐγὼ ὑμεῖς οὐ δύνασθε ἐλθεῖν;

37 Ἐν δὲ τῇ ἐσχάτῃ ἡμέρᾳ τῇ μεγάλῃ τῆς ἑορτῆς εἱστήκει ὁ Ἰησοῦς, καὶ ἔκραξεν λέγων·

Ἐάν τις διψᾷ ἐρχέσθω πρός με καὶ πινέτω. **38** ὁ πιστεύων εἰς ἐμέ, καθὼς εἶπεν ἡ γραφή, ποταμοὶ ἐκ τῆς κοιλίας αὐτοῦ ῥεύσουσιν ὕδατος ζῶντος.

39 τοῦτο δὲ εἶπεν περὶ τοῦ πνεύματος οὗ ἔμελλον λαμβάνειν οἱ πιστεύσαντες εἰς αὐτόν· οὔπω γὰρ ἦν πνεῦμα, ὅτι Ἰησοῦς οὐδέπω ἐδοξάσθη.

40 Ἐκ τοῦ ὄχλου οὖν ἀκούσαντες τῶν λόγων τούτων ἔλεγον·

Οὗτός ἐστιν ἀληθῶς ὁ προφήτης·

41 ἄλλοι ἔλεγον·

Οὗτός ἐστιν ὁ χριστός·

οἱ δὲ ἔλεγον·

Μὴ γὰρ ἐκ τῆς Γαλιλαίας ὁ χριστὸς ἔρχεται; **42** οὐχ ἡ γραφὴ εἶπεν ὅτι ἐκ τοῦ σπέρματος Δαυίδ, καὶ ἀπὸ Βηθλέεμ τῆς κώμης ὅπου ἦν Δαυίδ, ἔρχεται ὁ χριστός;

43 σχίσμα οὖν ἐγένετο ἐν τῷ ὄχλῳ δι' αὐτόν. **44** τινὲς δὲ ἤθελον ἐξ αὐτῶν πιάσαι αὐτόν, ἀλλ' οὐδεὶς ἐπέβαλεν ἐπ' αὐτὸν τὰς χεῖρας.

7:35 Therefore, the Jewish Officials said to themselves, "Where is this man about to go that we ourselves will not find him? He isn't about to go into the Diaspora among the Greeks, and to teach the Greeks, is he? (No!) **7:36** What is this word which he said: 'You will seek me and will not find, and where I myself am, you are not able to come'?" **7:37** Now, on the great last day of the Feast, Jesus had stood up and he shouted saying: "If any one thirsts, let him come to me and drink. **7:38** The one that keeps trusting in me, just as the Scripture said, 'rivers of living water will flow out of his innermost part.'" **7:39** And he spoke this concerning the Spirit, which the ones that trusted in him were about to receive. For the Spirit was not yet *present*, because Jesus was not yet glorified. **7:40** Therefore, *some* from the crowd, after hearing these words, began saying, "This one is truly the prophet!" **7:41** Others were saying, "This one is the Anointed One!" But some were saying, "The Anointed One surely does not come out of The Galilee, does he? (No!) **7:42** Didn't the Scripture say that from the seed of David, and from Bethlehem the village where David was, comes the Anointed One? (Yes!)" **7:43** Therefore, a division occurred in the crowd because of him. **7:44** Moreover, some from them were wanting to seize him, but no one laid hands on him.

7:45–8:1

7:45 Therefore, the officers went to the Chief Priests and Pharisees, and those *leaders* said to them, "Why did you not bring him?!" 7:46 The officers answered back, "Never ever did a person speak in this way!" 7:47 Therefore, the Pharisees answered back to them, "You yourselves haven't also been led astray, have you? (No!) 7:48 No one from the rulers trusted in him, or from the Pharisees, have they? (No!) 7:49 However, this crowd that doesn't know the law is accursed!" 7:50 Nicodemus says to them, the one that came to him earlier, since he was one of them, 7:51 "Our law doesn't judge the person, unless it hears first from him and knows what he was doing, does it? (No!)" 7:52 They answered back and said to him, "You yourself also aren't from The Galilee, are you? (No!) Search and see that a prophet is not raised up out of The Galilee." 7:53 And they left, each to his own home. 8:1 But Jesus went to the Mount of Olives.

8:2 Well, by early morning, he arrived again into the temple and all the people were coming to him and, after sitting down, he began teaching them. 8:3 So, the Scribes and the Pharisees bring a woman having been caught in adultery and, after they stood her up in the middle, 8:4 they began saying to him, "Teacher, this woman has been caught in the very act while committing adultery. 8:5 Moreover, in the law, Moses commanded us to stone ones such as these. Therefore, what do you yourself say?" 8:6 Additionally, they said this tempting him, in order that they would accuse him. But after Jesus bent down below, he began writing with his finger upon the ground. 8:7 So, as they kept on interrogating him, he stood up and said to them, "The sinless one among you, first let him throw a rock at her." 8:8 And again, after he stooped down, he wrote with his finger upon the ground. 8:9 Well, the ones that listened one by one began going out, starting from the elders and Jesus was left alone, the woman also being there in the middle. 8:10 So, after he stood up, Jesus said to her, "Woman, where are they? Did no one condemn you?" 8:11 Well, she said, "No one, Lord!" So Jesus said, "Neither then am I myself condemning you; go, from this moment sin no longer!"

8:12 Again, therefore, Jesus spoke to them saying, "I myself am the light of the world: The one that is following me will never ever walk in the darkness, but he will have the light of life." 8:13 Therefore, the Pharisees said to him, "You yourself are testifying about yourself; your testimony is not true." 8:14 Jesus answered back and said to them, "Even if I myself testify about myself, my testimony is true, because I know where I came from and where I am departing; but you yourselves do not know where I am coming from or where I am departing. 8:15 You yourselves are judging according to the flesh; I myself am not judging a single person. 8:16 Moreover, even if I myself judge, my judgment would be true, because I am not alone *in judging*, but *it is* I and the Father who sent me. 8:17 Furthermore, also in your law it has been written that the testimony of two people is true. 8:18 I myself am the one that is testifying about myself and the Father that sent me is testifying about me." 8:19 Therefore, they began saying to him, "Where is your Father?" Jesus answered back, "You neither know me, nor my Father; if you had known me, you would have known my Father also." 8:20 These words he spoke in the treasury while teaching in the temple; and no one seized him because his hour had not yet come. 8:21 Therefore, he said to them again, "I myself am departing and you will seek me, and in your sin you will die; for where I myself am departing, you yourselves are not able to go."

8:22 Therefore, the Jewish officials said, "He won't kill himself, will he, because he says, 'Where I myself am departing, you yourselves are not able to go'?" (No!) 8:23 And he proceeded saying to them, "You yourselves are from below; I myself am from above; you yourselves are from this world; I myself am not from this world." 8:24 Therefore, I said to you this: 'You will die in your sins; for if you do not trust that I myself am *the one*, you will die in your sins.'" 8:25 Therefore, they began saying to him, "You, who are you?" Jesus told them to begin with this: "Indeed, I am telling you. 8:26 I have many things about you to tell and to judge; but the one that sent me is true, and I myself, what I heard from him, these things I am speaking to the world." 8:27 They did not understand that he was speaking to them with reference to the Father. 8:28 Therefore, Jesus said, "Whenever you lift up the Son of Humanity, then you will know that I myself am *the one*, and by myself I do not do a single thing, but just as the Father taught me, I am speaking these things. 8:29 And the one that sent me is with me; he has not left me alone, because I myself am doing things pleasing to him, always!" 8:30 While speaking these things, many trusted in him. 8:31 Therefore, Jesus began saying to the Jewish Officials that had believed him, "If you yourselves remain in my word, you are truly my disciples; 8:32 and you will know the truth, and the truth will free you."

8:33 They answered back to him, "We are Abraham's seed and we have served no one ever; how *come* you are saying this: 'You will become free?'" 8:34 Jesus answered them, "Amen! Amen! I am saying to you this: 'Every one that is committing sin is a slave of sin. 8:35 Moreover, the slave does not remain in the house for ever; the son remains for ever. 8:36 Therefore, if the Son frees you, you will certainly be free. 8:37 I know that you are Abraham's seed; however, you are seeking to kill me, because my word is not making progress among you. 8:38 That which I have seen from the father I speak; therefore, you yourselves also are doing that which you heard from the father.» 8:39 They answered back and said to him, "Our father is Abraham." Jesus says to them, "If you were children of Abraham, you would be doing the works of Abraham. 8:40 Yet now you are seeking to kill me, a person who has spoken the truth to you, which I heard from God; Abraham did not do this. 8:41 You yourselves are doing the works of your father." They said to him, "We ourselves have not been born of out sexual immorality; we have one Father, God."

8:42 Jesus said to them, "If God were your Father, you would be loving me. For I myself came from God and I am present. Indeed, moreover, I have not come from myself, but that one sent me. 8:43 Why do you not understand my speaking? *It is* because you are not able to hear my word. 8:44 You yourselves are from the father, the devil, and you are wanting to do the desires of your father. That one was a murderer from the beginning, and does not stand in the truth, because there is no truth in him. Whenever he speaks a lie, he speaks from his own accord, because he is a liar, and the father of *lying*. 8:45 But myself, because I say the truth, you do not trust me. 8:46 Who from you accuses me of sin? If I say *the* truth, why do you yourselves not trust me? 8:47 The one that is from God hears the words of God; for this reason, you yourselves are not hearing, because you are not from God. 8:48 The Jewish Officials answered back and said to him, "We ourselves are speaking well that you yourself are a Samaritan and have a demon, aren't we? (Yes!) 8:49 Jesus answered back, "I myself do not have a demon; but I am honoring my Father, and you yourselves are dishonoring me!" 8:50 But I myself am not seeking my own glory; the one that is seeking *it* is also judging. 8:51 Amen! Amen! I am saying to you, If anyone keeps my word, he will never ever see death forever. 8:52 The Jewish Officials said to him, "Now we have realized that you have a demon. Abraham died, and the prophets, and you yourself are saying, 'If anyone keeps my word, he will never ever taste death forever.'

8:53 You aren't greater than our father Abraham, who died, are you? (No!) And the prophets died: You are making yourself whom?!"
8:54 Jesus answered back, "If I myself glorify myself, my glory is nothing; it is my Father that glorifies me, whom you yourselves say that he is your God; 8:55 and you have not known him; but I know him. And if I say that I do not know him, I will be like you, a liar. But I know him and I am keeping his word. 8:56 Abraham, your father, was overjoyed that he would see my day, and he saw it and rejoiced." 8:57 Therefore, the Jewish Officials said to him, "You are not yet fifty years old and you have seen Abraham?!" 8:58 Jesus said to them, "Amen! Amen! I am saying to you, before Abraham was, I am." 8:59 Therefore, they took up rocks in order that they would cast *them* at him; but Jesus hid himself and went out of the temple.

9:1 And as he was passing by, he saw a person blind from birth. 9:2 And his disciples asked him saying, "Our Master, who sinned, this one or his parents, that he would be born blind?" 9:3 Jesus answered back, "Neither this one sinned, nor his parents, but in order that the works of God would be made manifest in him, 9:4 we must be working the works of the one that sent me while it is day; the night is coming when no one is able to be working. 9:5 Whenever I am in the world, I am the light of the world." 9:6 After he said these things, he spit on the ground and made clay from the spit, and rubbed the clay upon his eyes, 9:7 and said to him, "Get going, wash in the pool of Siloam" (which is interpreted 'Having been sent'). Therefore, he departed and washed and came *back* seeing.

9:8 Therefore, the neighbors and the ones that were seeing him earlier, becasue he was a beggar, began saying, "Isn't this the sitting and begging one? (Yes.)" 9:9 Others kept saying this: "This is the one." Others were saying, "Surely not! Rather, he is like him." That one kept saying this: "I am he!" 9:10 Therefore, they began saying to him, "How were your eyes opened?" 9:11 That one answered back, "The person that is called 'Jesus' made clay, and rubbed my eyes, and said to me this: "Get going into Siloam and wash; so, after departing and washing, I regained sight!" 9:12 And they said to him, "Where is that one?" He says, "I don't know." 9:13 They begin bringing him to the Pharisees, the formerly blind one. 9:14 Moreover, it was Sabbath on the day which Jesus made the clay and opened his eyes. 9:15 Again, therefore, the Pharisees also began asking him how he regained sight. So he said said to them, "He put clay upon my eyes, and I washed, and I am seeing." 9:16 Therefore, some of the Pharisees began saying, "This one is not the person from God, because he is not keeping the Sabbath!" But others kept saying, "How is a sinful person able to be doing such signs as these?" And there was division among them.

9:17 Therefore, they say to the blind man again, "What are you yourself saying about him, that he opened your eyes?" Well, he said this: "He is the Prophet." 9:18 Therefore, concerning him the Jewish Officials did not trust that he was blind and regained sight, while they called the parents of him, the one that had regained sight, 9:19 and they asked them, saying: "Is this one your son, whom you yourselves are saying that he was born blind? How therefore is he seeing now?" 9:20 Therefore, his parents answered back and said, "We know that this one is our son and that he was born blind; 9:21 but how he is now seeing, we do not know, or who opened his eyes, we ourselves do know not; ask him, he is an adult, he himself will speak concerning himself!" 9:22 These things his parents said, because they were fearing the Jewish Officials, for already the Jewish Officials had agreed that, if anyone confessed him *to be* the Anointed One, he would be put out of the synagogue. 9:23 On account of this, his parents said this: "He is an adult; ask him." 9:24 Therefore, a second time they called the person who was blind and said to him, "Give glory to God! We ourselves know that this person is sinful." 9:25 Therefore, that one answered back, "If he is sinful, I do not know; one thing I know, that, although I was blind, now I see." 9:26 Therefore, they said to him, "What did he do to you? How did he open your eyes?" 9:27 He answered back to them, "I told you already and you did not hear; why do you want to hear *it* again? You yourselves wouldn't also want to become his disciples, would you? (Surely not!)"

9:28–37

9:28 They railed against him and said, "You yourself are a disciple of that one, but we ourselves are disciples of Moses! 9:29 We ourselves know that God has spoken to Moses, but, this one, we do not know where he is from." 9:30 The person answered back and said to them, "Indeed, in this *situation* the amazing thing is that you yourselves do not know where he is from, and he opened my eyes." 9:31 "We know that God does not hear sinners, but, if ever anyone is a worshipper of God and does his will, he hears him. 9:32 From the beginning of time, it was not heard that anyone opened the eyes of a person born blind. 9:33 If this one were not from God, he would not be able to do a single thing." 9:34 They answered back and said to him, "In sins you yourself were totally born, and you yourself are teaching us?!" And they threw him outside. 9:35 Jesus heard that they threw him outside; and after finding him, he said, "Are you yourself trusting in the Son of Humanity?" 9:36 That one answered and said, "And who is he, Lord, that I would trust in him?" 9:37 Jesus said to him, "Both you have seen him, and the one that is speaking with you is that one!"

9:38 So, he said, "Lord, I trust." And he bowed down to him. 9:39 And Jesus said, "For judgment I myself came into this world, in order that the ones not seeing would see and the ones seeing would become blind." 9:40 Those from the Pharisees that were with him heard these things, and said to him, "We ourselves also aren't blind, are we? (Surely not!)" 9:41 Jesus said to them, "If you were blind *(which you are not!)*, you would be having no sin. But now you are saying this: 'We are seeing'; your sin is remaining." 10:1 Amen! Amen! I say to you, "The one that is not entering through the door into the pen of the sheep, but is going up another way, that one is a thief and a robber. 10:2 But the one that is entering through the door is the shepherd of the sheep. 10:3 The doorkeeper continues opening *the door* for this one, and the sheep are listening for his voice and he begins calling his own sheep by name and continues leading them out. 10:4 Whenever he brings out all his own, he proceeds going before them, and the sheep continue following him, because they know his voice. 10:5 Moreover, they will not ever follow a stranger, but they will flee from him, because they do not know the voice of strangers." 10:6 Jesus spoke this proverb to them; but, those ones did not understand what it was which he kept saying to them.

10:7–21

7 Εἶπεν οὖν πάλιν αὐτοῖς ὁ Ἰησοῦς·

Ἀμὴν ἀμὴν λέγω ὑμῖν ὅτι ἐγώ εἰμι ἡ θύρα τῶν προβάτων. **8** πάντες ὅσοι ἦλθον πρὸ ἐμοῦ κλέπται εἰσὶν καὶ λῃσταί· ἀλλ' οὐκ ἤκουσαν αὐτῶν τὰ πρόβατα. **9** ἐγώ εἰμι ἡ θύρα· δι' ἐμοῦ ἐάν τις εἰσέλθῃ σωθήσεται καὶ εἰσελεύσεται καὶ ἐξελεύσεται καὶ νομὴν εὑρήσει. **10** ὁ κλέπτης οὐκ ἔρχεται εἰ μὴ ἵνα κλέψῃ καὶ θύσῃ καὶ ἀπολέσῃ· ἐγὼ ἦλθον ἵνα ζωὴν ἔχωσιν καὶ περισσὸν ἔχωσιν. **11** Ἐγώ εἰμι ὁ ποιμὴν ὁ καλός· ὁ ποιμὴν ὁ καλὸς τὴν ψυχὴν αὐτοῦ τίθησιν ὑπὲρ τῶν προβάτων· **12** ὁ μισθωτὸς καὶ οὐκ ὢν ποιμήν, οὗ οὐκ ἔστιν τὰ πρόβατα ἴδια, θεωρεῖ τὸν λύκον ἐρχόμενον καὶ ἀφίησιν τὰ πρόβατα καὶ φεύγει—καὶ ὁ λύκος ἁρπάζει αὐτὰ καὶ σκορπίζει— **13** ὅτι μισθωτός ἐστιν καὶ οὐ μέλει αὐτῷ περὶ τῶν προβάτων. **14** ἐγώ εἰμι ὁ ποιμὴν ὁ καλός, καὶ γινώσκω τὰ ἐμὰ καὶ γινώσκουσί με τὰ ἐμά, **15** καθὼς γινώσκει με ὁ πατὴρ κἀγὼ γινώσκω τὸν πατέρα, καὶ τὴν ψυχήν μου τίθημι ὑπὲρ τῶν προβάτων. **16** καὶ ἄλλα πρόβατα ἔχω ἃ οὐκ ἔστιν ἐκ τῆς αὐλῆς ταύτης· κἀκεῖνα δεῖ με ἀγαγεῖν, καὶ τῆς φωνῆς μου ἀκούσουσιν, καὶ γενήσονται μία ποίμνη, εἷς ποιμήν. **17** διὰ τοῦτό με ὁ πατὴρ ἀγαπᾷ ὅτι ἐγὼ τίθημι τὴν ψυχήν μου, ἵνα πάλιν λάβω αὐτήν. **18** οὐδεὶς αἴρει αὐτὴν ἀπ' ἐμοῦ, ἀλλ' ἐγὼ τίθημι αὐτὴν ἀπ' ἐμαυτοῦ. ἐξουσίαν ἔχω θεῖναι αὐτήν, καὶ ἐξουσίαν ἔχω πάλιν λαβεῖν αὐτήν· ταύτην τὴν ἐντολὴν ἔλαβον παρὰ τοῦ πατρός μου.

19 Σχίσμα πάλιν ἐγένετο ἐν τοῖς Ἰουδαίοις διὰ τοὺς λόγους τούτους. **20** ἔλεγον δὲ πολλοὶ ἐξ αὐτῶν·

Δαιμόνιον ἔχει καὶ μαίνεται· τί αὐτοῦ ἀκούετε;

21 ἄλλοι ἔλεγον·

Ταῦτα τὰ ῥήματα οὐκ ἔστιν δαιμονιζομένου· μὴ δαιμόνιον δύναται τυφλῶν ὀφθαλμοὺς ἀνοῖξαι;

10:7 Therefore, Jesus said to them again, "Amen! Amen! I say to you this: I am the door of the sheep. 10:8 All, as many as came before me, are thieves and robbers; but, the sheep did not hear them. 10:9 I myself am the door; if anyone enters in through me, he will be saved and will go in and will go out and will find pasture. 10:10 The thief is not coming except in order that he would steal and kill and destroy; I myself came in order that they would have life and would have *it* abundantly. 10:11 I myself am the good shepherd; the good shepherd continues putting forth his life for the sheep. 10:12 The hired hand, whose sheep are not his own, since he also is not a shepherd, begins seeing the wolf coming and starts leaving the sheep and continues fleeing—and the wolf begins snatching them and continues scattering *them*— 10:13 because he is a hired hand and does not care about the sheep. 10:14 I myself am the good shepherd, and I know my *sheep*, and my *sheep* know me, 10:15 just as the Father continues knowing me and I myself continue knowing the Father, and I continue putting forth my life for the sheep. 10:16 And I have other sheep, which are not from this pen; I must bring these also, and they will hear my voice, and there will be one flock, one shepherd. 10:17 On account of this, with respect to me the Father continues loving that I myself keep putting forth my life, in order that I would receive it again. 10:18 No one is taking it away from me, but I myself, I keep putting it forth by myself. I continue having authority to put it forth and again having authority to give it. I received this commandment from my Father." 10:19 Again a division occurred among the Jewish Officials because of these words. 10:20 Moreover, many of them kept saying, "He has a demon and is going mad! Why are you listening to him?!" 10:21 Others were saying: "These sayings are not from one being possessed by a demon. A demon cannot open the eyes of the blind, can it? (Surely not!)"

10:22 Then the Feast of the Dedication occurred in Jerusalem; it was winter, 10:23 and Jesus was walking about in the temple in Solomon's porch. 10:24 Therefore, the Jewish Officials circled around him and began saying to him, "How long until you take away our life? If you yourself are the Anointed One, tell us openly." 10:25 Jesus answered back to them, "I spoke to you, and you are not trusting: the works which I myself am doing in the name of my father, these *works* testify about me. 10:26 But you yourselves are not trusting, because you are not from my sheep. 10:27 My sheep keep listening to my voice, and I myself know them, and they continue following me, 10:28 and I am giving to them everlasting life, and they will never ever perish, and no one will snatch them out of my hand. 10:29 My Father, who has given *them* to me, is greater than all, and no one is able to be snatching *them* out of the Father's hand. 10:30 I and the Father, we are one."

10:31–42

31 Ἐβάστασαν οὖν πάλιν λίθους οἱ Ἰουδαῖοι ἵνα λιθάσωσιν αὐτόν.

32 ἀπεκρίθη αὐτοῖς ὁ Ἰησοῦς·

Πολλὰ ἔργα καλὰ ἔδειξα ὑμῖν ἐκ τοῦ πατρός· διὰ ποῖον αὐτῶν ἔργον ἐμὲ λιθάζετε;

33 ἀπεκρίθησαν αὐτῷ οἱ Ἰουδαῖοι·

Περὶ καλοῦ ἔργου οὐ λιθάζομέν σε ἀλλὰ περὶ βλασφημίας, καὶ ὅτι σὺ ἄνθρωπος ὢν ποιεῖς σεαυτὸν θεόν.

34 ἀπεκρίθη αὐτοῖς ὁ Ἰησοῦς·

Οὐκ ἔστιν γεγραμμένον ἐν τῷ νόμῳ ὑμῶν ὅτι Ἐγὼ εἶπα· Θεοί ἐστε; 35 εἰ ἐκείνους εἶπεν θεοὺς πρὸς οὓς ὁ λόγος τοῦ θεοῦ ἐγένετο, καὶ οὐ δύναται λυθῆναι ἡ γραφή, 36 ὃν ὁ πατὴρ ἡγίασεν καὶ ἀπέστειλεν εἰς τὸν κόσμον ὑμεῖς λέγετε ὅτι Βλασφημεῖς, ὅτι εἶπον· Υἱὸς τοῦ θεοῦ εἰμι;

37 εἰ οὐ ποιῶ τὰ ἔργα τοῦ πατρός μου, μὴ πιστεύετέ μοι· 38 εἰ δὲ ποιῶ, κἂν ἐμοὶ μὴ πιστεύητε τοῖς ἔργοις πιστεύετε, ἵνα γνῶτε καὶ γινώσκητε ὅτι ἐν ἐμοὶ ὁ πατὴρ κἀγὼ ἐν τῷ πατρί.

39 ἐζήτουν οὖν πάλιν αὐτὸν πιάσαι· καὶ ἐξῆλθεν ἐκ τῆς χειρὸς αὐτῶν.

40 Καὶ ἀπῆλθεν πάλιν πέραν τοῦ Ἰορδάνου εἰς τὸν τόπον ὅπου ἦν Ἰωάννης τὸ πρῶτον βαπτίζων, καὶ ἔμεινεν ἐκεῖ.

41 καὶ πολλοὶ ἦλθον πρὸς αὐτὸν καὶ ἔλεγον ὅτι

Ἰωάννης μὲν σημεῖον ἐποίησεν οὐδέν, πάντα δὲ ὅσα εἶπεν Ἰωάννης περὶ τούτου ἀληθῆ ἦν.

42 καὶ πολλοὶ ἐπίστευσαν εἰς αὐτὸν ἐκεῖ.

10:31 Therefore, the Jewish Officials picked up rocks again in order that they would stone him. 10:32 Jesus answered back to them, "Many good works I showed you from the Father; on account of what sort of work of these are you going stone me?" 10:33 The Jewish Officials answered back to him, "Concerning a good work, we are not stoning you, but rather concerning blasphemy and because you yourself, being a person, are making yourself God." 10:34 Jesus answered back to them, "Hasn't this been written in your law: 'I myself said: You are gods?' 10:35 If he called those to whom the word of God came 'gods', and the Scripture cannot be broken, 10:36 he whom the Father sanctified and sent into the world, *then why* are you yourselves saying this: 'You are blaspheming!' because I said, 'I am the Son of God'? 10:37 If I am not doing the works of my Father, do not trust me. 10:38 But if I am doing *them*, although you are not trusting me, trust the works, in order that you would come to know and continue knowing that the Father *is* in me and I myself *am* in the Father." 10:39 Therefore, they searched for him again to seize him; and he went out away from their reach. 10:40 And he departed again beyond the Jordan into the place where John was at first baptizing, and he stayed there. 10:41 And many came to him and they began saying this: "On the one hand, John made no sign, but everything, as much as John said about this one, was true." 10:42 And many trusted in him there.

11:1 Well, a certain man was sick, Lazarus from Bethany from the village of Mary and her sister Martha. 11:2 Moreover, it was Mary, the one that anointed the Lord with ointment and wiped his feet with her hair, whose brother, Lazarus, was sick. 11:3 Therefore, the sisters sent to him, saying, "Lord, look, the one whom you love is sick." 11:4 But, after hearing, Jesus said, "This sickness does not result in death, but is for the glory of God, in order that the Son of God would be glorified through it." 11:5 Well, Jesus loved Martha and her sister and Lazarus. 11:6 Therefore, as he heard that he was sick, indeed, then he remained in the place he was for two days. 11:7 Next, after this, he says to the disciples, "Let's go into Judea again." 11:8 The disciples say to him, "Our Teacher, currently the Jewish Officials were seeking to stone you, and again you are going there?!" 11:9 Jesus answered back, "Are there not twelve hours in the day? (Yes!) If someone walks during the day, he doesn't stumble, because he sees the light of this world. 11:10 But if someone walks at night, he stumbles, because the light is not in him."

11:11 He said these things, and after this he says to them, "Lazarus, our friend, has fallen asleep, but I am going in order that I would wake him up." 11:12 The disciples, therefore, said to him, "Lord, if he has fallen asleep, he will recover." 11:13 Well, Jesus had spoken about his death; but those ones supposed that he was speaking about sleep. 11:14 Then, therefore, Jesus said to them openly, "Lazarus died. 11:15 And I am glad for your sakes, in order that you would believe, that I was not there; nevertheless, let us go to him." 11:16 Therefore, Thomas, the one being called Didymus, said to his fellow-disciples, "Let us ourselves go also, in order that we would die with him." 11:17 So, after going, Jesus found him already being in the tomb for four days already. 11:18 Well, Bethany was near Jerusalem, about fifteen stadia away. 11:19 Furthermore, many from the Jews had come to Martha and Mary, in order to console them concerning their brother. 11:20 Therefore, Martha, as she heard that Jesus was coming, met him; but Mary continued sitting in the house.

11:21 Therefore, Martha said to Jesus, "Lord, if you had been here, my brother would not have died. **11:22** And now I know that however much you ask of God, God will give to you." **11:23** Jesus says to her, "Your brother will rise again." **11:24** Martha says to him, "I know that he will rise again in the resurrection at the last day." **11:25** Jesus said to her, "I myself am the resurrection and the life; the one that believes in me, even if he dies, he will live, **11:26** and everyone that lives and believes in me will never ever die in the age to come. Are you believing this?" **11:27** She says to him, "Yes, Lord; I myself have believed that you yourself are the Anointed One, the Son of God, the One that comes into the world." **11:28** And when she said this, she went away and called Mary her sister secretly, saying, "The Teacher is present and calls you." **11:29** Well, that one, as she heard it, arose quickly and began going to him. **11:30** Furthermore, Jesus had not yet come into the village, but was still in the place where Martha met him. **11:31** Therefore, the Jews that were with her in the house and consoling her, after seeing that Mary rose up quickly and went out, followed her, supposing that she was going to the tomb in order to weep there. **11:32** Therefore, Mary, as she came where Jesus was, after seeing him, fell down at his feet, saying to him, "Lord, if you had been here, my brother would not have died." **11:33** So then, as Jesus saw her weeping and the Jews coming with her weeping, he was deeply moved in his spirit and was troubled,

11:34–42

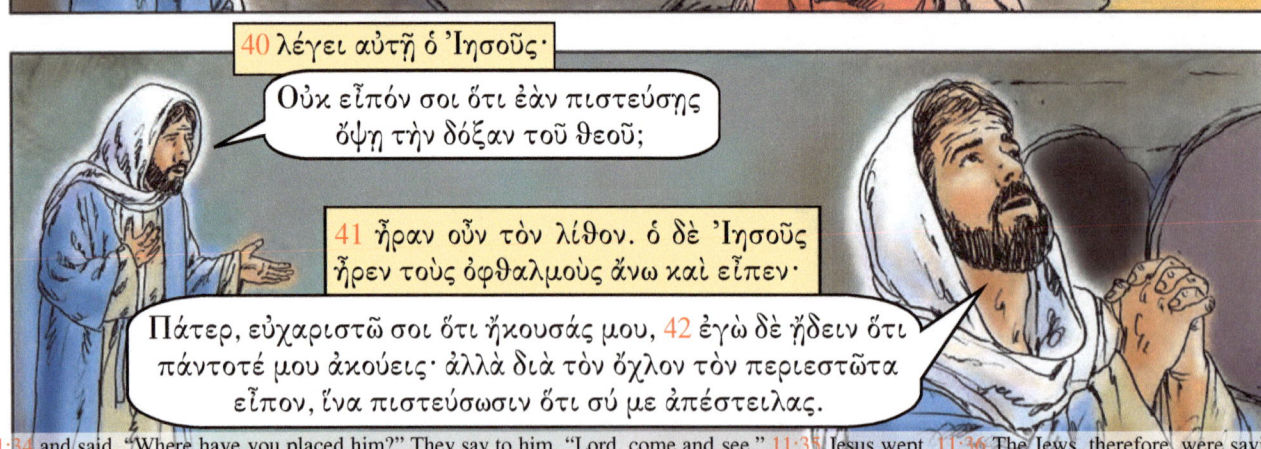

11:34 and said, "Where have you placed him?" They say to him, "Lord, come and see." 11:35 Jesus wept. 11:36 The Jews, therefore, were saying, "See how he was loving him!" 11:37 But some of them said, "Wasn't this guy that opened the eyes of the one that was blind able to make it that this man also would not die? (Surely yes!)" 11:38 Therefore, Jesus, again deeply moved in himself, goes to the tomb. It was a cave and a stone was lying against it. 11:39 Jesus says, "Take away the stone." The sister of the one having died, Martha, says to him, "Lord, he smells already; for it's the fourth day." 11:40 Jesus says to her, "Didn't I say to you, that, if you believe, you would see the glory of God? (Yes!)" 11:41 Therefore, they took away the stone. Then Jesus lifted his eyes upwards and said, "Father, I give thanks to you that you heard me. 11:42 Furthermore, I myself knew that you always heard me; but because of the crowd that stands around, I said it in order that they would believe that you yourself sent me."

11:43–53

43 καὶ ταῦτα εἰπὼν φωνῇ μεγάλῃ ἐκραύγασεν·

Λάζαρε, δεῦρο ἔξω.

44 ἐξῆλθεν ὁ τεθνηκὼς δεδεμένος τοὺς πόδας καὶ τὰς χεῖρας κειρίαις, καὶ ἡ ὄψις αὐτοῦ σουδαρίῳ περιεδέδετο.

λέγει αὐτοῖς ὁ Ἰησοῦς·

Λύσατε αὐτὸν καὶ ἄφετε αὐτὸν ὑπάγειν.

45 Πολλοὶ οὖν ἐκ τῶν Ἰουδαίων, οἱ ἐλθόντες πρὸς τὴν Μαριὰμ καὶ θεασάμενοι ἃ ἐποίησεν, ἐπίστευσαν εἰς αὐτόν· 46 τινὲς δὲ ἐξ αὐτῶν ἀπῆλθον πρὸς τοὺς Φαρισαίους καὶ εἶπαν αὐτοῖς ἃ ἐποίησεν Ἰησοῦς. 47 συνήγαγον οὖν οἱ ἀρχιερεῖς καὶ οἱ Φαρισαῖοι συνέδριον, καὶ ἔλεγον·

Τί ποιοῦμεν ὅτι οὗτος ὁ ἄνθρωπος πολλὰ ποιεῖ σημεῖα; 48 ἐὰν ἀφῶμεν αὐτὸν οὕτως, πάντες πιστεύσουσιν εἰς αὐτόν, καὶ ἐλεύσονται οἱ Ῥωμαῖοι καὶ ἀροῦσιν ἡμῶν καὶ τὸν τόπον καὶ τὸ ἔθνος.

49 εἷς δέ τις ἐξ αὐτῶν Καϊάφας, ἀρχιερεὺς ὢν τοῦ ἐνιαυτοῦ ἐκείνου, εἶπεν αὐτοῖς·

Ὑμεῖς οὐκ οἴδατε οὐδέν, 50 οὐδὲ λογίζεσθε ὅτι συμφέρει ὑμῖν ἵνα εἷς ἄνθρωπος ἀποθάνῃ ὑπὲρ τοῦ λαοῦ καὶ μὴ ὅλον τὸ ἔθνος ἀπόληται.

51 τοῦτο δὲ ἀφ' ἑαυτοῦ οὐκ εἶπεν, ἀλλὰ ἀρχιερεὺς ὢν τοῦ ἐνιαυτοῦ ἐκείνου ἐπροφήτευσεν ὅτι ἔμελλεν Ἰησοῦς ἀποθνῄσκειν ὑπὲρ τοῦ ἔθνους,

52 καὶ οὐχ ὑπὲρ τοῦ ἔθνους μόνον, ἀλλ' ἵνα καὶ τὰ τέκνα τοῦ θεοῦ τὰ διεσκορπισμένα συναγάγῃ εἰς ἕν. 53 ἀπ' ἐκείνης οὖν τῆς ἡμέρας ἐβουλεύσαντο ἵνα ἀποκτείνωσιν αὐτόν.

11:43 And after he had spoken these things, he cried with a loud voice, "Lazarus, come here, outside!" 11:44 The one that had died came out, having been bound hand and foot with grave-clothes, and his face had been wrapped with a face-cloth. Jesus says to them, "Loosen him and let him go." 11:45 Therefore, many from the Jews, the ones that came to Mary and beheld that which he did, believed in him; 11:46 but some of them departed to the Pharisees and told them the things which Jesus did. 11:47 Therefore, the chief priests and the Pharisees gathered a council and were saying, "What are we doing, because this person is accomplishing many signs?! 11:48 If we allow him to act like this, all people will believe in him, and the Romans will come and take away both our position and our nation." 11:49 But a certain one of them, Caiaphas, being high priest during that year, said to them, "You yourselves know nothing at all, 11:50 nor do you consider that it is beneficial for you that one person should die for the people and not the whole nation perish." 11:51 Well, he said this not from himself, but, being high priest during that year, he prophesied that Jesus was about to die for the nation; 11:52 and not for the nation only, but in order that he would also gather together the scattered children of God into one body. 11:53 Therefore, from that day they took counsel in order to kill him.

11:54–12:4

54 Ὁ οὖν Ἰησοῦς οὐκέτι παρρησίᾳ περιεπάτει ἐν τοῖς Ἰουδαίοις, ἀλλὰ ἀπῆλθεν ἐκεῖθεν εἰς τὴν χώραν ἐγγὺς τῆς ἐρήμου, εἰς Ἐφραὶμ λεγομένην πόλιν, κἀκεῖ ἔμεινεν μετὰ τῶν μαθητῶν.

55 Ἦν δὲ ἐγγὺς τὸ πάσχα τῶν Ἰουδαίων, καὶ ἀνέβησαν πολλοὶ εἰς Ἱεροσόλυμα ἐκ τῆς χώρας πρὸ τοῦ πάσχα ἵνα ἁγνίσωσιν ἑαυτούς. 56 ἐζήτουν οὖν τὸν Ἰησοῦν καὶ ἔλεγον μετ' ἀλλήλων ἐν τῷ ἱερῷ ἑστηκότες·

Τί δοκεῖ ὑμῖν; ὅτι οὐ μὴ ἔλθῃ εἰς τὴν ἑορτήν;

57 δεδώκεισαν δὲ οἱ ἀρχιερεῖς καὶ οἱ Φαρισαῖοι ἐντολὰς ἵνα ἐάν τις γνῷ ποῦ ἐστιν μηνύσῃ, ὅπως πιάσωσιν αὐτόν.

Chapter 12

12:1 Ὁ οὖν Ἰησοῦς πρὸ ἓξ ἡμερῶν τοῦ πάσχα ἦλθεν εἰς Βηθανίαν, ὅπου ἦν Λάζαρος, ὃν ἤγειρεν ἐκ νεκρῶν Ἰησοῦς. 2 ἐποίησαν οὖν αὐτῷ δεῖπνον ἐκεῖ, καὶ ἡ Μάρθα διηκόνει, ὁ δὲ Λάζαρος εἷς ἦν ἐκ τῶν ἀνακειμένων σὺν αὐτῷ·

3 ἡ οὖν Μαριὰμ λαβοῦσα λίτραν μύρου νάρδου πιστικῆς πολυτίμου ἤλειψεν τοὺς πόδας τοῦ Ἰησοῦ καὶ ἐξέμαξεν ταῖς θριξὶν αὐτῆς τοὺς πόδας αὐτοῦ·

ἡ δὲ οἰκία ἐπληρώθη ἐκ τῆς ὀσμῆς τοῦ μύρου. 4 λέγει δὲ Ἰούδας ὁ Ἰσκαριώτης εἷς τῶν μαθητῶν αὐτοῦ, ὁ μέλλων αὐτὸν παραδιδόναι·

11:54 Jesus, therefore, no longer walked openly among the Jews, but he departed from there into the country near the wilderness, into a city called Ephraim; and there he tarried with the disciples. 11:55 Well, the Passover of the Jews was at hand, and many went up to Jerusalem from the country before the Passover in order to purify themselves. 11:56 Therefore, they were searching for Jesus and were speaking with one another standing in the temple: "Why do you think that he would never ever come to the Feast?" 11:57 Moreover, the chief priests and the Pharisees had given commands, that, if someone knew where he was, they should give report, in order that they would seize him. 12:1 Therefore, Jesus, six days before the Passover, came to Bethany, where Lazarus was from, whom Jesus raised from the dead. 12:2 So, they made him supper there and Martha was serving; additionally, Lazarus was one among the ones that reclined to eat with him. 12:3 Mary, therefore, took a pound of ointment of pure nard, very precious, and anointed the feet of Jesus and wiped his feet with her hair; and the house was filled with the odor of the ointment. 12:4 But Judas Iscariot, one of his disciples, the one about to betray him, says,

5 Διὰ τί τοῦτο τὸ μύρον οὐκ ἐπράθη τριακοσίων δηναρίων καὶ ἐδόθη πτωχοῖς;

6 εἶπεν δὲ τοῦτο οὐχ ὅτι περὶ τῶν πτωχῶν ἔμελεν αὐτῷ, ἀλλ' ὅτι κλέπτης ἦν καὶ τὸ γλωσσόκομον ἔχων τὰ βαλλόμενα ἐβάσταζεν. 7 εἶπεν οὖν ὁ Ἰησοῦς·

Ἄφες αὐτήν, ἵνα εἰς τὴν ἡμέραν τοῦ ἐνταφιασμοῦ μου τηρήσῃ αὐτό· 8 τοὺς πτωχοὺς γὰρ πάντοτε ἔχετε μεθ' ἑαυτῶν, ἐμὲ δὲ οὐ πάντοτε ἔχετε.

9 Ἔγνω οὖν ὄχλος πολὺς ἐκ τῶν Ἰουδαίων ὅτι ἐκεῖ ἐστιν, καὶ ἦλθον οὐ διὰ τὸν Ἰησοῦν μόνον, ἀλλ' ἵνα καὶ τὸν Λάζαρον ἴδωσιν ὃν ἤγειρεν ἐκ νεκρῶν. 10 ἐβουλεύσαντο δὲ οἱ ἀρχιερεῖς ἵνα καὶ τὸν Λάζαρον ἀποκτείνωσιν, 11 ὅτι πολλοὶ δι' αὐτὸν ὑπῆγον τῶν Ἰουδαίων καὶ ἐπίστευον εἰς τὸν Ἰησοῦν.

12 Τῇ ἐπαύριον ὁ ὄχλος πολὺς ὁ ἐλθὼν εἰς τὴν ἑορτήν, ἀκούσαντες ὅτι ἔρχεται ὁ Ἰησοῦς εἰς Ἱεροσόλυμα, 13 ἔλαβον τὰ βαΐα τῶν φοινίκων καὶ ἐξῆλθον εἰς ὑπάντησιν αὐτῷ, καὶ ἐκραύγαζον·

14 εὑρὼν δὲ ὁ Ἰησοῦς ὀνάριον ἐκάθισεν ἐπ' αὐτό, καθώς ἐστιν γεγραμμένον·

15 Μὴ φοβοῦ, θυγάτηρ Σιών· ἰδοὺ ὁ βασιλεύς σου ἔρχεται, καθήμενος ἐπὶ πῶλον ὄνου.

Ὡσαννά, εὐλογημένος ὁ ἐρχόμενος ἐν ὀνόματι κυρίου, καὶ ὁ βασιλεὺς τοῦ Ἰσραήλ.

12:5 "For what reason was not this ointment sold for three hundred denarii and given to the poor?" 12:6 Moreover, he said this, not because he cared for the poor, but because he was a thief and, while having the money purse, he was removing that which was being cast in. 12:7 Jesus, therefore, said, "Permit her, in order the she would keep it for the day of my burial; 12:8 for the poor you always have with you, but me you do not always have." 12:9 Therefore, a great crowd from the Jews learned that he was there and they came, not for Jesus' sake only, but in order that also they would see Lazarus, whom he raised from the dead. 12:10 But the chief priests took counsel in order also to kill Lazarus, 12:11 because on account of him, many of the Jews were going and believing in Jesus. 12:12 On the next day, the great crowd that had come to the Feast, after hearing that Jesus was coming to Jerusalem, 12:13 took the branches of the palm trees and went forth to meet him and were crying out, "Hosanna, Blessed is the one that comes in the name of the Lord, even the King of Israel!" 12:14 Well, after Jesus found a young donkey, he sat upon it, just as it is written: 12:15 "Fear not, daughter of Zion! Behold, your King comes, sitting on a donkey's colt."

12:16 (These things his disciples did not understand at the first, but when Jesus was glorified, at that time they remembered that these things were written about him and that they did these things to him.) 12:17 Therefore, the crowd that was with him when he called Lazarus from the tomb and raised him from the dead was bearing testimony. 12:18 For this reason also, the crowd met him, because they heard this, namely, that he had accomplished this sign. 12:19 The Pharisees, therefore ,said among themselves, "Observe that you were not benefiting a single thing! Look, the world has gone after him!" 12:20 Well, there were certain Greeks from the ones that were going up in order to worship at the Feast. 12:21 These, therefore, came to Philip, the one from Bethsaida of Galilee, and began asking him saying, "Sir, we are wanting to see Jesus." 12:22 Philip goes and tells Andrew; Andrew and Philip go and they speak to Jesus. 12:23 Then Jesus answers back to them, saying, "The hour has come that the Son of Humanity would be glorified. 12:24 Amen! Amen! I say to you, unless the grain of wheat falling into the earth dies, it remains by itself alone; but if it dies, it bears much fruit. 12:25 The one that loves his life loses it, and the one that hates his life in this world will keep it for everlasting life.

12:26 If any one serves me, let him keep following me and where I myself am, there also will my servant be; if any one serves me, the Father will honor him. 12:27 Now my soul has become troubled, and what should I say? 'Father, save me from this hour!' But on account of this, I came for this hour. 12:28 Father, glorify your name." There came, therefore, a voice from heaven, "I have both glorified it and I will glorify it again." 12:29 Therefore, the crowd that stood by and heard it were saying that it had thundered; others were saying, "An angel has spoken to him!" 12:30 Jesus answered back and said, "This voice has not come for my sake, but for your sakes. 12:31 Now is the judgment of this world; now will the ruler of this world be cast out. 12:32 And I myself, if I am lifted up from the earth, will draw all to myself." 12:33 But he was speaking this signifying by what manner of death he was about to die. 12:34 The crowd, therefore, answered back to him, "We ourselves have heard from the law that the Anointed One remains into the age to come, and how do you yourself say, "The Son of Humanity must be lifted up? Who is this Son of Humanity?" 12:35 Jesus, therefore, said to them, "Yet for a little while the light is among you. Walk when you have the light, in order that darkness would not overtake you, and the one that walks in the darkness does not know where he goes. 12:36 While you have the light, believe in the light, in order that you would become sons of light." Jesus spoke these things and, after departing, he hid himself from them. 12:37 But although he had done so many signs before them, yet they were not believing in him, 12:38 in order that the word of Isaiah the prophet would be fulfilled which he spoke, "Lord, who believed our report? And to whom was the arm of the Lord revealed?"

12:38–50

38 ἵνα ὁ λόγος Ἠσαΐου τοῦ προφήτου πληρωθῇ ὃν εἶπεν·

Κύριε, τίς ἐπίστευσεν τῇ ἀκοῇ ἡμῶν; καὶ ὁ βραχίων κυρίου τίνι ἀπεκαλύφθη;

39 διὰ τοῦτο οὐκ ἠδύναντο πιστεύειν ὅτι πάλιν εἶπεν Ἠσαΐας·

40 Τετύφλωκεν αὐτῶν τοὺς ὀφθαλμοὺς καὶ ἐπώρωσεν αὐτῶν τὴν καρδίαν, ἵνα μὴ ἴδωσιν τοῖς ὀφθαλμοῖς καὶ νοήσωσιν τῇ καρδίᾳ καὶ στραφῶσιν, καὶ ἰάσομαι αὐτούς.

41 ταῦτα εἶπεν Ἠσαΐας ὅτι εἶδεν τὴν δόξαν αὐτοῦ, καὶ ἐλάλησεν περὶ αὐτοῦ. 42 ὅμως μέντοι καὶ ἐκ τῶν ἀρχόντων πολλοὶ ἐπίστευσαν εἰς αὐτόν,

ἀλλὰ διὰ τοὺς Φαρισαίους οὐχ ὡμολόγουν ἵνα μὴ ἀποσυνάγωγοι γένωνται, 43 ἠγάπησαν γὰρ τὴν δόξαν τῶν ἀνθρώπων μᾶλλον ἤπερ τὴν δόξαν τοῦ θεοῦ. 44 Ἰησοῦς δὲ ἔκραξεν καὶ εἶπεν·

Ὁ πιστεύων εἰς ἐμὲ οὐ πιστεύει εἰς ἐμὲ ἀλλὰ εἰς τὸν πέμψαντά με, 45 καὶ ὁ θεωρῶν ἐμὲ θεωρεῖ τὸν πέμψαντά με. 46 ἐγὼ φῶς εἰς τὸν κόσμον ἐλήλυθα, ἵνα πᾶς ὁ πιστεύων εἰς ἐμὲ ἐν τῇ σκοτίᾳ μὴ μείνῃ.

47 καὶ ἐάν τίς μου ἀκούσῃ τῶν ῥημάτων καὶ μὴ φυλάξῃ, ἐγὼ οὐ κρίνω αὐτόν, οὐ γὰρ ἦλθον ἵνα κρίνω τὸν κόσμον ἀλλ' ἵνα σώσω τὸν κόσμον. 48 ὁ ἀθετῶν ἐμὲ καὶ μὴ λαμβάνων τὰ ῥήματά μου ἔχει τὸν κρίνοντα αὐτόν· ὁ λόγος ὃν ἐλάλησα ἐκεῖνος κρινεῖ αὐτὸν ἐν τῇ ἐσχάτῃ ἡμέρᾳ· 49 ὅτι ἐγὼ ἐξ ἐμαυτοῦ οὐκ ἐλάλησα, ἀλλ' ὁ πέμψας με πατὴρ αὐτός μοι ἐντολὴν δέδωκεν τί εἴπω καὶ τί λαλήσω. 50 καὶ οἶδα ὅτι ἡ ἐντολὴ αὐτοῦ ζωὴ αἰώνιός ἐστιν. ἃ οὖν ἐγὼ λαλῶ, καθὼς εἴρηκέν μοι ὁ πατήρ, οὕτως λαλῶ.

12:38 in order that the word of Isaiah the prophet would be fulfilled which he spoke, "Lord, who believed our report? And to whom was the arm of the Lord revealed?" 12:39 For this reason they were not able to believe, because again Isaiah said, 12:40 "He has blinded their eyes and he hardened their heart, lest they would see with their eyes and perceive with their heart and would turn and I will heal them." 12:41 These things Isaiah said because he saw his glory and he spoke concerning him. 12:42 Nevertheless, yet even many of the rulers believed in him, but because of the Pharisees they were not confessing, lest they would become removed from the synagogue, 12:43 for they loved the glory from people more than the glory from God. 12:44 And Jesus cried and said, "The one that believes in me, believes not in me, but in the One that sent me. 12:45 And the one that beholds me beholds the One that sent me. 12:46 I myself have come as light into the world, in order that the one that believes in me would not remain in the darkness. 12:47 And if someone hears my words and does not keep them, I myself am not judging him; for I did not come in order to judge the world, but in order to save the world. 12:48 The one that is rejecting me and is not receiving my words has one that judges him; the word which I spoke, that will judge him in the last day, 12:49 because I myself did not speak from myself, but the Father that sent me has given a commandment to me, what I should say and what I should speak. 12:50 And I know that his commandment is everlasting life. Therefore, that which I myself am speaking, just as the Father has spoken to me, thus I am speaking."

Chapter 13

13:1 Πρὸ δὲ τῆς ἑορτῆς τοῦ πάσχα εἰδὼς ὁ Ἰησοῦς ὅτι ἦλθεν αὐτοῦ ἡ ὥρα ἵνα μεταβῇ ἐκ τοῦ κόσμου τούτου πρὸς τὸν πατέρα ἀγαπήσας τοὺς ἰδίους τοὺς ἐν τῷ κόσμῳ εἰς τέλος ἠγάπησεν αὐτούς. 2 καὶ δείπνου γινομένου, τοῦ διαβόλου ἤδη βεβληκότος εἰς τὴν καρδίαν ἵνα παραδοῖ αὐτὸν Ἰούδας Σίμωνος Ἰσκαριώτου, 3 εἰδὼς ὅτι πάντα ἔδωκεν αὐτῷ ὁ πατὴρ εἰς τὰς χεῖρας, καὶ ὅτι ἀπὸ θεοῦ ἐξῆλθεν καὶ πρὸς τὸν θεὸν ὑπάγει,

4 ἐγείρεται ἐκ τοῦ δείπνου καὶ τίθησιν τὰ ἱμάτια καὶ λαβὼν λέντιον διέζωσεν ἑαυτόν·

5 εἶτα βάλλει ὕδωρ εἰς τὸν νιπτῆρα,

καὶ ἤρξατο νίπτειν τοὺς πόδας τῶν μαθητῶν καὶ ἐκμάσσειν τῷ λεντίῳ ᾧ ἦν διεζωσμένος.

13:1 Well, before the Feast of the Passover, Jesus, knowing that his hour had come, that he would depart from this world to his Father, having loved his own that were in the world, he loved them completely. 13:2 And while dinner was occurring, the devil having already put into the heart of Judas Iscariot, son of Simon, that he betray him, 13:3 knowing that the Father had given all the things into his hands and that he had come from God and was departing to God, 13:4 he arises from the dinner and sets aside his garments and, after taking a towel, he girded himself. 13:5 Next, he pours water into the basin and began to wash the disciples' feet and to wipe them with the towel with which he was girded.

13:6–18a

13:6 So, he comes to Simon Peter. He says to him, "Lord, are you yourself washing my feet?" 13:7 Jesus answered back and said to him, "That which I myself am doing you yourself are not comprehending; but you will understand after these things." 13:8 Peter says to him, "You will never ever wash my feet in the age to come!" Jesus answered back to him, "If I don't wash you, you have no part with me!" 13:9 Simon Peter says to him, "Lord, not my feet only, but also my hands and my head." 13:10 Jesus says to him, "The one that has bathed has no need except to wash his feet; otherwise, he is wholly clean and you yourselves are clean, but not all of you." 13:11 For he knew the one that was betraying him; on account of this, he said this: "Not all of you are clean." 13:12 Therefore, when he had washed their feet and taken his garments and sat down, again he said to them, "Do you know what I have done for you? 13:13 You yourselves call me, 'Teacher,' and, 'Lord' and you speak properly, for I am. 13:14 If, then, I myself the Lord and the Teacher have washed your feet, you yourselves also ought to wash one another's feet; 13:15 for I gave you an example, in order that, just as I myself did to you, you also would do. 13:16 Amen! Amen! I say to you, a servant is not greater than his master, nor is a delegate greater than the one that sent him. 13:17 If you know these things, you are blessed if you do them. 13:18 I am not speaking about all of you; I myself know which ones I have chosen;

13:27–38

27 καὶ μετὰ τὸ ψωμίον τότε εἰσῆλθεν εἰς ἐκεῖνον ὁ Σατανᾶς. λέγει οὖν αὐτῷ ὁ Ἰησοῦς·

"Ὃ ποιεῖς ποίησον τάχιον.

28 τοῦτο δὲ οὐδεὶς ἔγνω τῶν ἀνακειμένων πρὸς τί εἶπεν αὐτῷ· 29 τινὲς γὰρ ἐδόκουν, ἐπεὶ τὸ γλωσσόκομον εἶχεν Ἰούδας, ὅτι λέγει αὐτῷ ὁ Ἰησοῦς· Ἀγόρασον ὧν χρείαν ἔχομεν εἰς τὴν ἑορτήν, ἢ τοῖς πτωχοῖς ἵνα τι δῷ.

30 λαβὼν οὖν τὸ ψωμίον ἐκεῖνος ἐξῆλθεν εὐθύς. ἦν δὲ νύξ.

31 Ὅτε οὖν ἐξῆλθεν λέγει Ἰησοῦς·

Νῦν ἐδοξάσθη ὁ υἱὸς τοῦ ἀνθρώπου, καὶ ὁ θεὸς ἐδοξάσθη ἐν αὐτῷ· 32 εἰ ὁ θεὸς ἐδοξάσθη ἐν αὐτῷ, καὶ ὁ θεὸς δοξάσει αὐτὸν ἐν αὐτῷ, καὶ εὐθὺς δοξάσει αὐτόν. 33 τεκνία, ἔτι μικρὸν μεθ' ὑμῶν εἰμι· ζητήσετέ με, καὶ καθὼς εἶπον τοῖς Ἰουδαίοις ὅτι Ὅπου ἐγὼ ὑπάγω ὑμεῖς οὐ δύνασθε ἐλθεῖν, καὶ ὑμῖν λέγω ἄρτι. 34 ἐντολὴν καινὴν δίδωμι ὑμῖν ἵνα ἀγαπᾶτε ἀλλήλους, καθὼς ἠγάπησα ὑμᾶς ἵνα καὶ ὑμεῖς ἀγαπᾶτε ἀλλήλους. 35 ἐν τούτῳ γνώσονται πάντες ὅτι ἐμοὶ μαθηταί ἐστε, ἐὰν ἀγάπην ἔχητε ἐν ἀλλήλοις.

36 Λέγει αὐτῷ Σίμων Πέτρος·

Κύριε, ποῦ ὑπάγεις;

ἀπεκρίθη Ἰησοῦς·

Ὅπου ὑπάγω οὐ δύνασαί μοι νῦν ἀκολουθῆσαι, ἀκολουθήσεις δὲ ὕστερον.

37 λέγει αὐτῷ ὁ Πέτρος·

Κύριε, διὰ τί οὐ δύναμαί σοι ἀκολουθῆσαι ἄρτι; τὴν ψυχήν μου ὑπὲρ σοῦ θήσω.

38 ἀποκρίνεται Ἰησοῦς·

Τὴν ψυχήν σου ὑπὲρ ἐμοῦ θήσεις;

ἀμὴν ἀμὴν λέγω σοι, οὐ μὴ ἀλέκτωρ φωνήσῃ ἕως οὗ ἀρνήσῃ με τρίς.

13:27 And after the morsel, then Satan entered into that one. Jesus, therefore, says to him, "That which you are doing, do quickly." 13:28 Well, none of the ones reclining at the table knew this, that is, for what reason he spoke to him. 13:29 For some were thinking, since Judas was holding the money box, that Jesus said to him, 'Buy what things we have need for the Feast;' or, for the poor, that he give something. 13:30 Therefore, having received the morsel, that one went out immediately. Moreover, it was night. 13:31 When, therefore, he went out, Jesus says, "Now the Son of Humanity is glorified, and God is glorified in him; 13:32 If God is glorified in him, God will also glorify him in himself, and immediately will he glorify him. 13:33 Little children, yet a little longer I am with you. You will seek me, and just as I said to the Jewish Officials this: 'Where I go, you are not able to come,' also to you I say it now. 13:34 A new commandment I give to you, that you love one another, just as I have loved you, in order that you yourselves also love one another. 13:35 By this all will know that you are my disciples, if you have love among one another." 13:36 Simon Peter says to him, "Lord, where are you departing?" Jesus answered back, "Where I am departing you are not able to follow now; but you will follow afterwards." 13:37 Peter says to him, "Lord, for what reason am I not able to follow you now? My life I will lay down for you!" 13:38 Jesus answers back, "Your life you will lay down for me! Amen! Amen! I say to you, the rooster will surely not crow until you deny me three times.

14:1 Let not your heart continue being troubled; continue believing in God and believing in me. 14:2 In my Father's house are many rooms; moreover, if it were not so, I would have told you, because I am going to prepare a place for you. 14:3 And if I go and prepare a place for you, I am coming again and I will take you for myself, in order that, where I am, you yourselves would also be. 14:4 And where I myself depart, you know the way." 14:5 Thomas says to him, "Lord, we do not know where you are departing; how are we able to know the way?!" 14:6 Jesus says to him, "I myself am the way and the truth and the life; no one comes to the Father except through me. 14:7 If you had known me, you would also have known my Father; from now on you know him and have seen him." 14:8 Philip says to him, "Lord, show us the Father and it is sufficient for us."

14:9–22

9 λέγει αὐτῷ ὁ Ἰησοῦς·

Τοσούτῳ χρόνῳ μεθ' ὑμῶν εἰμι καὶ οὐκ ἔγνωκάς με, Φίλιππε; ὁ ἑωρακὼς ἐμὲ ἑώρακεν τὸν πατέρα· πῶς σὺ λέγεις· Δεῖξον ἡμῖν τὸν πατέρα; **10** οὐ πιστεύεις ὅτι ἐγὼ ἐν τῷ πατρὶ καὶ ὁ πατὴρ ἐν ἐμοί ἐστιν; τὰ ῥήματα ἃ ἐγὼ λέγω ὑμῖν ἀπ' ἐμαυτοῦ οὐ λαλῶ, ὁ δὲ πατὴρ ἐν ἐμοὶ μένων ποιεῖ τὰ ἔργα αὐτοῦ. **11** πιστεύετέ μοι ὅτι ἐγὼ ἐν τῷ πατρὶ καὶ ὁ πατὴρ ἐν ἐμοί· εἰ δὲ μή, διὰ τὰ ἔργα αὐτὰ πιστεύετε. **12** ἀμὴν ἀμὴν λέγω ὑμῖν, ὁ πιστεύων εἰς ἐμὲ τὰ ἔργα ἃ ἐγὼ ποιῶ κἀκεῖνος ποιήσει, καὶ μείζονα τούτων ποιήσει, ὅτι ἐγὼ πρὸς τὸν πατέρα πορεύομαι· **13** καὶ ὅ τι ἂν αἰτήσητε ἐν τῷ ὀνόματί μου τοῦτο ποιήσω, ἵνα δοξασθῇ ὁ πατὴρ ἐν τῷ υἱῷ· **14** ἐάν τι αἰτήσητέ με ἐν τῷ ὀνόματί μου ἐγὼ ποιήσω. **15** Ἐὰν ἀγαπᾶτέ με, τὰς ἐντολὰς τὰς ἐμὰς τηρήσετε· **16** κἀγὼ ἐρωτήσω τὸν πατέρα καὶ ἄλλον παράκλητον δώσει ὑμῖν ἵνα ᾖ μεθ' ὑμῶν εἰς τὸν αἰῶνα, **17** τὸ πνεῦμα τῆς ἀληθείας, ὃ ὁ κόσμος οὐ δύναται λαβεῖν, ὅτι οὐ θεωρεῖ αὐτὸ οὐδὲ γινώσκει· ὑμεῖς γινώσκετε αὐτό, ὅτι παρ' ὑμῖν μένει καὶ ἐν ὑμῖν ἔσται. **18** Οὐκ ἀφήσω ὑμᾶς ὀρφανούς, ἔρχομαι πρὸς ὑμᾶς. **19** ἔτι μικρὸν καὶ ὁ κόσμος με οὐκέτι θεωρεῖ, ὑμεῖς δὲ θεωρεῖτέ με, ὅτι ἐγὼ ζῶ καὶ ὑμεῖς ζήσετε. **20** ἐν ἐκείνῃ τῇ ἡμέρᾳ γνώσεσθε ὑμεῖς ὅτι ἐγὼ ἐν τῷ πατρί μου καὶ ὑμεῖς ἐν ἐμοὶ κἀγὼ ἐν ὑμῖν. **21** ὁ ἔχων τὰς ἐντολάς μου καὶ τηρῶν αὐτὰς ἐκεῖνός ἐστιν ὁ ἀγαπῶν με·

ὁ δὲ ἀγαπῶν με ἀγαπηθήσεται ὑπὸ τοῦ πατρός μου, κἀγὼ ἀγαπήσω αὐτὸν καὶ ἐμφανίσω αὐτῷ ἐμαυτόν.

22 λέγει αὐτῷ Ἰούδας, οὐχ ὁ Ἰσκαριώτης·

Κύριε, τί γέγονεν ὅτι ἡμῖν μέλλεις ἐμφανίζειν σεαυτὸν καὶ οὐχὶ τῷ κόσμῳ;

14:9 Jesus says to him, "For such a long time I am with you and haven't you known me, Philip? (Surely yes!) The one that has seen me has seen the Father; how are you saying, 'Show us the Father'?! **14:10** Are you not believing that I am in the Father, and the Father is in me? (Surely yes!) The words which I myself am speaking to you I am not speaking from myself, but the Father remaining in me accomplishes his deeds. **14:11** Believe me that I myself am in the Father and the Father in me; but if not, then on account of the deeds themselves, believe! **14:12** Amen! Amen! I say to you, the one that believes in me, the deeds that I myself accomplish, that one will also accomplish, and greater deeds than these will he accomplish, because I myself am going to the Father. **14:13** And whatever you ask in my name, I will do this, in order that the Father would be glorified in the Son. **14:14** If you ask anything in my name, I will do *it*. **14:15** If you love me, you will keep my commandments. **14:16** And I will ask the Father, and he will give you another Comforter, in order that he would be with you into the age to come, **14:17** the Spirit of truth, whom the world is not able to receive, because it neither sees nor knows him. You yourselves know him, because he remains with you and will be among you. **14:18** I will not leave you without family; I am coming to you. **14:19** Yet a little while and the world sees me no longer, but you yourselves see me, because I myself am living and you yourselves will live. **14:20** In that day you yourselves will know that I myself am in my Father, and you in me and I in you. **14:21** The one that has my commandments and keeps them, that one is the one that loves me; moreover, the one that loves me will be loved by my Father, and I myself will love him and will make myself visible to him." **14:22** Judas (not Iscariot) says to him, "Lord, what has happened that you are about to make yourself visible to us and not to the world?"

23 ἀπεκρίθη Ἰησοῦς καὶ εἶπεν αὐτῷ·

Ἐάν τις ἀγαπᾷ με τὸν λόγον μου τηρήσει, καὶ ὁ πατήρ μου ἀγαπήσει αὐτόν, καὶ πρὸς αὐτὸν ἐλευσόμεθα καὶ μονὴν παρ' αὐτῷ ποιησόμεθα. 24 ὁ μὴ ἀγαπῶν με τοὺς λόγους μου οὐ τηρεῖ· καὶ ὁ λόγος ὃν ἀκούετε οὐκ ἔστιν ἐμὸς ἀλλὰ τοῦ πέμψαντός με πατρός. 25 Ταῦτα λελάληκα ὑμῖν παρ' ὑμῖν μένων· 26 ὁ δὲ παράκλητος, τὸ πνεῦμα τὸ ἅγιον ὃ πέμψει ὁ πατὴρ ἐν τῷ ὀνόματί μου, ἐκεῖνος ὑμᾶς διδάξει πάντα καὶ ὑπομνήσει ὑμᾶς πάντα ἃ εἶπον ὑμῖν. 27 εἰρήνην ἀφίημι ὑμῖν, εἰρήνην τὴν ἐμὴν δίδωμι ὑμῖν· οὐ καθὼς ὁ κόσμος δίδωσιν ἐγὼ δίδωμι ὑμῖν. μὴ ταρασσέσθω ὑμῶν ἡ καρδία μηδὲ δειλιάτω. 28 ἠκούσατε ὅτι ἐγὼ εἶπον ὑμῖν· Ὑπάγω καὶ ἔρχομαι πρὸς ὑμᾶς. εἰ ἠγαπᾶτέ με ἐχάρητε ἄν, ὅτι πορεύομαι πρὸς τὸν πατέρα, ὅτι ὁ πατὴρ μείζων μού ἐστιν. 29 καὶ νῦν εἴρηκα ὑμῖν πρὶν γενέσθαι, ἵνα ὅταν γένηται πιστεύσητε. 30 οὐκέτι πολλὰ λαλήσω μεθ' ὑμῶν, ἔρχεται γὰρ ὁ τοῦ κόσμου ἄρχων· καὶ ἐν ἐμοὶ οὐκ ἔχει οὐδέν, 31 ἀλλ' ἵνα γνῷ ὁ κόσμος ὅτι ἀγαπῶ τὸν πατέρα, καὶ καθὼς ἐνετείλατό μοι ὁ πατὴρ οὕτως ποιῶ. Ἐγείρεσθε, ἄγωμεν ἐντεῦθεν.

Chapter 15

15:1 Ἐγώ εἰμι ἡ ἄμπελος ἡ ἀληθινή, καὶ ὁ πατήρ μου ὁ γεωργός ἐστιν· 2 πᾶν κλῆμα ἐν ἐμοὶ μὴ φέρον καρπὸν αἴρει αὐτό, καὶ πᾶν τὸ καρπὸν φέρον καθαίρει αὐτὸ ἵνα καρπὸν πλείονα φέρῃ. 3 ἤδη ὑμεῖς καθαροί ἐστε διὰ τὸν λόγον ὃν λελάληκα ὑμῖν· 4 μείνατε ἐν ἐμοί, κἀγὼ ἐν ὑμῖν. καθὼς τὸ κλῆμα οὐ δύναται καρπὸν φέρειν ἀφ' ἑαυτοῦ ἐὰν μὴ μένῃ ἐν τῇ ἀμπέλῳ, οὕτως οὐδὲ ὑμεῖς ἐὰν μὴ ἐν ἐμοὶ μένητε. 5 ἐγώ εἰμι ἡ ἄμπελος, ὑμεῖς τὰ κλήματα. ὁ μένων ἐν ἐμοὶ κἀγὼ ἐν αὐτῷ οὗτος φέρει καρπὸν πολύν, ὅτι χωρὶς ἐμοῦ οὐ δύνασθε ποιεῖν οὐδέν. 6 ἐὰν μή τις μένῃ ἐν ἐμοί, ἐβλήθη ἔξω ὡς τὸ κλῆμα καὶ ἐξηράνθη, καὶ συνάγουσιν αὐτὰ καὶ εἰς τὸ πῦρ βάλλουσιν καὶ καίεται. 7 ἐὰν μείνητε ἐν ἐμοὶ καὶ τὰ ῥήματά μου ἐν ὑμῖν μείνῃ, ὃ ἐὰν θέλητε αἰτήσασθε καὶ γενήσεται ὑμῖν· 8 ἐν τούτῳ ἐδοξάσθη ὁ πατήρ μου ἵνα καρπὸν πολὺν φέρητε καὶ γένησθε ἐμοὶ μαθηταί. 9 καθὼς ἠγάπησέν με ὁ πατήρ, κἀγὼ ὑμᾶς ἠγάπησα, μείνατε ἐν τῇ ἀγάπῃ τῇ ἐμῇ. 10 ἐὰν τὰς ἐντολάς μου τηρήσητε, μενεῖτε ἐν τῇ ἀγάπῃ μου, καθὼς ἐγὼ τὰς ἐντολὰς τοῦ πατρός μου τετήρηκα καὶ μένω αὐτοῦ ἐν τῇ ἀγάπῃ. 11 ταῦτα λελάληκα ὑμῖν ἵνα ἡ χαρὰ ἡ ἐμὴ ἐν ὑμῖν ᾖ καὶ ἡ χαρὰ ὑμῶν πληρωθῇ. 12 Αὕτη ἐστὶν ἡ ἐντολὴ ἡ ἐμὴ ἵνα ἀγαπᾶτε ἀλλήλους καθὼς ἠγάπησα ὑμᾶς· 13 μείζονα ταύτης ἀγάπην οὐδεὶς ἔχει, ἵνα τις τὴν ψυχὴν αὐτοῦ θῇ ὑπὲρ τῶν φίλων αὐτοῦ. 14 ὑμεῖς φίλοι μού ἐστε ἐὰν ποιῆτε ἃ ἐγὼ ἐντέλλομαι ὑμῖν. 15 οὐκέτι λέγω ὑμᾶς δούλους, ὅτι ὁ δοῦλος οὐκ οἶδεν τί ποιεῖ αὐτοῦ ὁ κύριος· ὑμᾶς δὲ εἴρηκα φίλους, ὅτι πάντα ἃ ἤκουσα παρὰ τοῦ πατρός μου ἐγνώρισα ὑμῖν. 16 οὐχ ὑμεῖς με ἐξελέξασθε, ἀλλ' ἐγὼ ἐξελεξάμην ὑμᾶς, καὶ ἔθηκα ὑμᾶς ἵνα ὑμεῖς ὑπάγητε καὶ καρπὸν φέρητε καὶ ὁ καρπὸς ὑμῶν μένῃ, ἵνα ὅ τι ἂν αἰτήσητε τὸν πατέρα ἐν τῷ ὀνόματί μου δῷ ὑμῖν. 17 ταῦτα ἐντέλλομαι ὑμῖν ἵνα ἀγαπᾶτε ἀλλήλους.

14:23 Jesus answered back and said to him, "If someone loves me he will keep my word, and my Father will love him, and we will come to him and make a dwelling with him. 14:24 The one that is not loving me does not keep my words; and the word which you hear is not mine but the Father's that sent me. 14:25 These things have I spoken to you while remaining with you. 14:26 But the Comforter, the Holy Spirit, whom the Father will send in my name, that one will teach you all things and will remind you of all the things which I spoke to you. 14:27 Peace I leave with you, my peace I give to you; not just as the world gives, I am giving to you. Let not your heart be troubled, nor let it be fearful. 14:28 You heard that I myself said to you, 'I am going away and I am coming to you.' If you were loving me, you would be rejoicing, because I am going to the Father, because the Father is greater than I. 14:29 And now I have told you before it happens, in order that, when it happens, you would believe. 14:30 I will no longer speak with you about many things, for the ruler of the world is coming; and he has nothing against me; 14:31 but in order that the world would know that I love the Father, and just as the Father commanded me, thus I am doing. Arise! Let us go forth! 15:1 I myself am the true vine and my Father is the vinedresser. 15:2 Every branch in me that is not bearing fruit, he takes it away; and every one that is bearing fruit, he prunes it, in order that it would bear more fruit. 15:3 Already, you yourselves are clean because of the word which I have spoken to you. 15:4 Abide in me, and I in you. As the branch cannot bear fruit of itself unless it abides in the vine, so neither can you, unless you abide in me. 15:5 I myself am the vine; you are the branches. The one that remains in me, and I in him, this one bears much fruit, because without me you are not able to accomplish a single thing. 15:6 If someone does not remain in me, he was cast outside as a branch and withered; and they gather them and cast them into the fire and he is burned. 15:7 If you remain in me and my words remain in you, whatever you want, ask and it will happen for you. 15:8 In this, my Father is glorified, that you bear much fruit and become my disciples. 15:9 Just as the Father loved me and I myself loved you, remain in my love. 15:10 If you keep my commandments, you will remain in my love, just as I myself have kept my Father's commandments and remain in his love. 15:11 These things have I spoken to you, in order that my joy would be in you and your joy would be made full. 15:12 This is my commandment, that you love one another just as I loved you. 15:13 Greater love has no man than this, that someone lay down his life for his friends. 15:14 You yourselves are my friends if you do that which I myself am commanding you. 15:15 No longer am I calling you servants because the servant does not know what his master is doing; but, I have called you friends because all things, which I heard from my Father, I made known to you. 15:16 You yourselves did not choose me, but I myself chose you and appointed you, in order that you would go and bear fruit and your fruit would remain, in order that whatever you ask the Father in my name, he would give it you. 15:17 These things I am commanding you, in order that you would love one another.

18 Εἰ ὁ κόσμος ὑμᾶς μισεῖ, γινώσκετε ὅτι ἐμὲ πρῶτον ὑμῶν μεμίσηκεν. 19 εἰ ἐκ τοῦ κόσμου ἦτε, ὁ κόσμος ἂν τὸ ἴδιον ἐφίλει· ὅτι δὲ ἐκ τοῦ κόσμου οὐκ ἐστέ, ἀλλ᾽ ἐγὼ ἐξελεξάμην ὑμᾶς ἐκ τοῦ κόσμου, διὰ τοῦτο μισεῖ ὑμᾶς ὁ κόσμος. 20 μνημονεύετε τοῦ λόγου οὗ ἐγὼ εἶπον ὑμῖν· Οὐκ ἔστιν δοῦλος μείζων τοῦ κυρίου αὐτοῦ· εἰ ἐμὲ ἐδίωξαν, καὶ ὑμᾶς διώξουσιν· εἰ τὸν λόγον μου ἐτήρησαν, καὶ τὸν ὑμέτερον τηρήσουσιν. 21 ἀλλὰ ταῦτα πάντα ποιήσουσιν εἰς ὑμᾶς διὰ τὸ ὄνομά μου, ὅτι οὐκ οἴδασιν τὸν πέμψαντά με. 22 εἰ μὴ ἦλθον καὶ ἐλάλησα αὐτοῖς, ἁμαρτίαν οὐκ εἴχοσαν· νῦν δὲ πρόφασιν οὐκ ἔχουσιν περὶ τῆς ἁμαρτίας αὐτῶν. 23 ὁ ἐμὲ μισῶν καὶ τὸν πατέρα μου μισεῖ. 24 εἰ τὰ ἔργα μὴ ἐποίησα ἐν αὐτοῖς ἃ οὐδεὶς ἄλλος ἐποίησεν, ἁμαρτίαν οὐκ εἴχοσαν· νῦν δὲ καὶ ἑωράκασιν καὶ μεμισήκασιν καὶ ἐμὲ καὶ τὸν πατέρα μου. 25 ἀλλ᾽ ἵνα πληρωθῇ ὁ λόγος ὁ ἐν τῷ νόμῳ αὐτῶν γεγραμμένος ὅτι Ἐμίσησάν με δωρεάν. 26 Ὅταν ἔλθῃ ὁ παράκλητος ὃν ἐγὼ πέμψω ὑμῖν παρὰ τοῦ πατρός, τὸ πνεῦμα τῆς ἀληθείας ὃ παρὰ τοῦ πατρὸς ἐκπορεύεται, ἐκεῖνος μαρτυρήσει περὶ ἐμοῦ· 27 καὶ ὑμεῖς δὲ μαρτυρεῖτε, ὅτι ἀπ᾽ ἀρχῆς μετ᾽ ἐμοῦ ἐστε.

Chapter 16

16:1 Ταῦτα λελάληκα ὑμῖν ἵνα μὴ σκανδαλισθῆτε. 2 ἀποσυναγώγους ποιήσουσιν ὑμᾶς· ἀλλ᾽ ἔρχεται ὥρα ἵνα πᾶς ὁ ἀποκτείνας ὑμᾶς δόξῃ λατρείαν προσφέρειν τῷ θεῷ. 3 καὶ ταῦτα ποιήσουσιν ὅτι οὐκ ἔγνωσαν τὸν πατέρα οὐδὲ ἐμέ. 4 ἀλλὰ ταῦτα λελάληκα ὑμῖν ἵνα ὅταν ἔλθῃ ἡ ὥρα αὐτῶν μνημονεύητε αὐτῶν ὅτι ἐγὼ εἶπον ὑμῖν. Ταῦτα δὲ ὑμῖν ἐξ ἀρχῆς οὐκ εἶπον, ὅτι μεθ᾽ ὑμῶν ἤμην. 5 νῦν δὲ ὑπάγω πρὸς τὸν πέμψαντά με καὶ οὐδεὶς ἐξ ὑμῶν ἐρωτᾷ με· Ποῦ ὑπάγεις; 6 ἀλλ᾽ ὅτι ταῦτα λελάληκα ὑμῖν ἡ λύπη πεπλήρωκεν ὑμῶν τὴν καρδίαν. 7 ἀλλ᾽ ἐγὼ τὴν ἀλήθειαν λέγω ὑμῖν, συμφέρει ὑμῖν ἵνα ἐγὼ ἀπέλθω. ἐὰν γὰρ μὴ ἀπέλθω, ὁ παράκλητος οὐ μὴ ἔλθῃ πρὸς ὑμᾶς· ἐὰν δὲ πορευθῶ, πέμψω αὐτὸν πρὸς ὑμᾶς. 8 καὶ ἐλθὼν ἐκεῖνος ἐλέγξει τὸν κόσμον περὶ ἁμαρτίας καὶ περὶ δικαιοσύνης καὶ περὶ κρίσεως· 9 περὶ ἁμαρτίας μέν, ὅτι οὐ πιστεύουσιν εἰς ἐμέ· 10 περὶ δικαιοσύνης δέ, ὅτι πρὸς τὸν πατέρα ὑπάγω καὶ οὐκέτι θεωρεῖτέ με· 11 περὶ δὲ κρίσεως, ὅτι ὁ ἄρχων τοῦ κόσμου τούτου κέκριται. 12 Ἔτι πολλὰ ἔχω ὑμῖν λέγειν, ἀλλ᾽ οὐ δύνασθε βαστάζειν ἄρτι· 13 ὅταν δὲ ἔλθῃ ἐκεῖνος, τὸ πνεῦμα τῆς ἀληθείας, ὁδηγήσει ὑμᾶς ἐν τῇ ἀληθείᾳ πάσῃ, οὐ γὰρ λαλήσει ἀφ᾽ ἑαυτοῦ, ἀλλ᾽ ὅσα ἀκούσει λαλήσει, καὶ τὰ ἐρχόμενα ἀναγγελεῖ ὑμῖν. 14 ἐκεῖνος ἐμὲ δοξάσει, ὅτι ἐκ τοῦ ἐμοῦ λήμψεται καὶ ἀναγγελεῖ ὑμῖν. 15 πάντα ὅσα ἔχει ὁ πατὴρ ἐμά ἐστιν· διὰ τοῦτο εἶπον ὅτι ἐκ τοῦ ἐμοῦ λαμβάνει καὶ ἀναγγελεῖ ὑμῖν. 16 Μικρὸν καὶ οὐκέτι θεωρεῖτέ με, καὶ πάλιν μικρὸν καὶ ὄψεσθέ με.

15:18 If the world hates you, know that it has hated me foremost before you. 15:19 If you were from the world, the world would be loving you as its own; but because you are not of the world, but I myself chose you from the world, for this reason the world hates you. 15:20 Remember the word that I spoke to you: 'A servant is not greater than his master'; if they persecuted me, they will also persecute you; if they kept my word, they will also keep yours. 15:21 But all these things will they do to you because of my name, because they do not know the One that sent me. 15:22 If I had not come and spoken to them, they would not have sin; but now they have no excuse for their sin. 15:23 The one that hates me also hates my Father. 15:24 If I had not accomplished among them the works which no one else accomplished, they would not have sin; but now they have both seen and hated both me and my Father. 15:25 But *this occurred* in order that the word would be fulfilled that has been written in their law, namely, this, 'They hated me without a cause.' 15:26 When the Comforter comes, whom I myself will send to you from the Father, namely, the Spirit of truth, which proceeds from the Father, that one will bear witness concerning me. 15:27 And you yourselves are also bearing witness, because you are with me from the beginning. 16:1 These things have I spoken to you, in order that you would not stumble. 16:2 They will put you out of the synagogues; but the hour is coming that everyone that kills you will suppose that he is offering service to God. 16:3 And they will do these things because they knew neither the Father nor me. 16:4 But I have spoken these things to you, in order that when their hour comes, you would remember them, that I myself spoke to you. But I did not speak these things to you from the beginning because I was with you. 16:5 But now I am departing to the One that sent me and no one from you asks me, 'Where are you departing?' 16:6 But because I have spoken these things to you, sorrow has filled your heart. 16:7 Nevertheless, I myself am speaking the truth to you; it is beneficial for you that I myself go away. For unless I go away, the Comforter will never ever come to you; but if I go, I will send him to you. 16:8 And after coming, that one will convict the world concerning sin and concerning righteousness and concerning judgment: 16:9 Indeed, concerning sin because they are not trusting in me; 16:10 Moreover, concerning righteousness, because I am departing to the Father and you are no longer beholding me; 16:11 finally, concerning judgment, because the ruler of this world has been judged. 16:12 I have still many things to say to you, but you are not able to bear them now;. 16:13 but, when that one comes, the Spirit of truth, he will guide you into all the truth, for he will not speak from himself, but as much as he will hear, he will speak and he will announce to you the things that are coming. 16:14 That one will glorify me because he will take from what is mine and will announce it to you. 16:15 All things, as much as the Father has, are mine; for this reason, I said that he takes from what is mine and will announce it to you. 16:16 A little while and no longer are you beholding me; and again a little while and you will see me."

16:17 Therefore, the ones from his disciples said to one another, "What is this that he says to us, 'A little while and you are not beholding me; and again a little while and you will see me'; and, 'Because I am departing to the Father'?" 16:18 Therefore, they kept saying, 'What is this that he says, 'A little while'? We do not know what he is saying." 16:19 Jesus knew that they were wanting to ask him and he said to them, "Do you search among yourselves concerning this that I said, 'A little while and you are not beholding me, and again a little while and you will see me'?" 16:20 Amen! Amen! I say to you that you yourselves will weep and lament, but the world will rejoice; you yourselves will be sorrowful, but your sorrow will become joy! 16:21 A woman, when she gives birth, has sorrow because her hour came; but when she bears the child, she no longer remembers the anguish because of the joy that a human was born into the world. 16:22 And you yourselves, therefore, now have sorrow; but I will see you again and your heart will rejoice and no one takes away your joy from you. 16:23 And in that day you will not ask me about a single thing. Amen! Amen! I say to you, if you will ask the Father for anything, he will give it to you in my name. 16:24 Until now, you have not asked for a single thing in my name; ask and you will receive, in order that your joy would be made full. 16:25 These things I have spoken to you in sophisticated sayings; the hour is coming when I will no more speak to you in sophisticated sayings, but I will tell you plainly about the Father. 16:26 In that day you will ask in my name, and I do not say to you that I myself will ask the Father concerning you; 16:27 for the Father himself loves you, because you have loved me and have believed that I myself came forth from God. 16:28 I came forth from the Father and I have come into the world; again, I am leaving the world and I am going to the Father."

29 Λέγουσιν οἱ μαθηταὶ αὐτοῦ·

Ἴδε νῦν ἐν παρρησίᾳ λαλεῖς, καὶ παροιμίαν οὐδεμίαν λέγεις. 30 νῦν οἴδαμεν ὅτι οἶδας πάντα καὶ οὐ χρείαν ἔχεις ἵνα τίς σε ἐρωτᾷ· ἐν τούτῳ πιστεύομεν ὅτι ἀπὸ θεοῦ ἐξῆλθες.

31 ἀπεκρίθη αὐτοῖς Ἰησοῦς·

Ἄρτι πιστεύετε;

32 ἰδοὺ ἔρχεται ὥρα καὶ ἐλήλυθεν ἵνα σκορπισθῆτε ἕκαστος εἰς τὰ ἴδια κἀμὲ μόνον ἀφῆτε· καὶ οὐκ εἰμὶ μόνος, ὅτι ὁ πατὴρ μετ' ἐμοῦ ἐστιν. 33 ταῦτα λελάληκα ὑμῖν ἵνα ἐν ἐμοὶ εἰρήνην ἔχητε· ἐν τῷ κόσμῳ θλῖψιν ἔχετε, ἀλλὰ θαρσεῖτε, ἐγὼ νενίκηκα τὸν κόσμον.

Chapter 17

17:1 Ταῦτα ἐλάλησεν Ἰησοῦς, καὶ ἐπάρας τοὺς ὀφθαλμοὺς αὐτοῦ εἰς τὸν οὐρανὸν εἶπεν·

Πάτερ, ἐλήλυθεν ἡ ὥρα· δόξασόν σου τὸν υἱόν, ἵνα ὁ υἱὸς δοξάσῃ σέ, 2 καθὼς ἔδωκας αὐτῷ ἐξουσίαν πάσης σαρκός, ἵνα πᾶν ὃ δέδωκας αὐτῷ δώσῃ αὐτοῖς ζωὴν αἰώνιον. 3 αὕτη δέ ἐστιν ἡ αἰώνιος ζωὴ ἵνα γινώσκωσι σὲ τὸν μόνον ἀληθινὸν θεὸν καὶ ὃν ἀπέστειλας Ἰησοῦν Χριστόν. 4 ἐγώ σε ἐδόξασα ἐπὶ τῆς γῆς, τὸ ἔργον τελειώσας ὃ δέδωκάς μοι ἵνα ποιήσω· 5 καὶ νῦν δόξασόν με σύ, πάτερ, παρὰ σεαυτῷ τῇ δόξῃ ᾗ εἶχον πρὸ τοῦ τὸν κόσμον εἶναι παρὰ σοί. 6 Ἐφανέρωσά σου τὸ ὄνομα τοῖς ἀνθρώποις οὓς ἔδωκάς μοι ἐκ τοῦ κόσμου. σοὶ ἦσαν κἀμοὶ αὐτοὺς ᶠ ἔδωκας, καὶ τὸν λόγον σου τετήρηκαν. 7 νῦν ἔγνωκαν ὅτι πάντα ὅσα δέδωκάς μοι παρὰ σοῦ εἰσιν· 8 ὅτι τὰ ῥήματα ἃ ἔδωκάς μοι δέδωκα αὐτοῖς, καὶ αὐτοὶ ἔλαβον καὶ ἔγνωσαν ἀληθῶς ὅτι παρὰ σοῦ ἐξῆλθον, καὶ ἐπίστευσαν ὅτι σύ με ἀπέστειλας. 9 ἐγὼ περὶ αὐτῶν ἐρωτῶ· οὐ περὶ τοῦ κόσμου ἐρωτῶ ἀλλὰ περὶ ὧν δέδωκάς μοι, ὅτι σοί εἰσιν, 10 καὶ τὰ ἐμὰ πάντα σά ἐστιν καὶ τὰ σὰ ἐμά, καὶ δεδόξασμαι ἐν αὐτοῖς. 11 καὶ οὐκέτι εἰμὶ ἐν τῷ κόσμῳ, καὶ αὐτοὶ ἐν τῷ κόσμῳ εἰσίν, κἀγὼ πρὸς σὲ ἔρχομαι. πάτερ ἅγιε, τήρησον αὐτοὺς ἐν τῷ ὀνόματί σου ᾧ δέδωκάς μοι, ἵνα ὦσιν ἓν καθὼς ἡμεῖς. 12 ὅτε ἤμην μετ' αὐτῶν ἐγὼ ἐτήρουν αὐτοὺς ἐν τῷ ὀνόματί σου ᾧ δέδωκάς μοι, καὶ ἐφύλαξα, καὶ οὐδεὶς ἐξ αὐτῶν ἀπώλετο εἰ μὴ ὁ υἱὸς τῆς ἀπωλείας, ἵνα ἡ γραφὴ πληρωθῇ.

16:29 His disciples say, "Look, now you are talking clearly and you are not speaking in sophisticated sayings. 16:30 Now we know that you know all things and you have no need that someone should ask you; by this we believe that you came forth from God." 16:31 Jesus answered back to them, "Now are you believing? 16:32 Behold, the hour is coming and has come that you will be scattered, each one to his own, and you will leave me alone; and I am not alone because the Father is with me. 16:33 These things have I spoken to you, in order that in me you would have peace. In the world you are having trouble, but be courageous, I myself have overcome the world!" 17:1 Jesus spoke these things, and lifting up his eyes to heaven, he said, "Father, the hour has come; glorify your Son, in order that the Son would glorify you, 17:2 just as you gave him authority over all flesh, in order that everyone whom you have given to him, he would give to them everlasting life. 17:3 And this is everlasting life, that they would know you, the only true God, and him whom you sent, Jesus, the Anointed One. 17:4 I myself glorified you on the earth, having accomplished that which you have given to me that I would do. 17:5 And now, Father, you glorify me with your own glory, which I was having with you before the world existed. 17:6 I manifested your name to the people whom you gave me from the world. They were yours, and you gave them to me; and they have kept your word. 17:7 Now they know that all things, as much as you have given to me, are from you, 17:8 because the words which you gave me I have given to them and they themselves received and knew truly that I came forth from you and they believed that you yourself sent me. 17:9 Concerning them, I myself am asking; I am not asking concerning the world, but concerning those whom you have given me, because they are yours, 17:10 and all things that are mine are yours, and your things are mine, and I am glorified in them. 17:11 And I am no longer in the world, and they themselves are in the world, and I myself am coming to you. Holy Father, keep them in your name, which you have given to me, in order that they would be one, just as we are. 17:12 When I was with them, I myself kept them in your name which you have given me, and I guarded, and not one of them perished except the son of perdition, in order that the Scripture would be fulfilled.

13 νῦν δὲ πρὸς σὲ ἔρχομαι, καὶ ταῦτα λαλῶ ἐν τῷ κόσμῳ ἵνα ἔχωσιν τὴν χαρὰν τὴν ἐμὴν πεπληρωμένην ἐν ἑαυτοῖς. 14 ἐγὼ δέδωκα αὐτοῖς τὸν λόγον σου, καὶ ὁ κόσμος ἐμίσησεν αὐτούς, ὅτι οὐκ εἰσὶν ἐκ τοῦ κόσμου καθὼς ἐγὼ οὐκ εἰμὶ ἐκ τοῦ κόσμου. 15 οὐκ ἐρωτῶ ἵνα ἄρῃς αὐτοὺς ἐκ τοῦ κόσμου ἀλλ᾽ ἵνα τηρήσῃς αὐτοὺς ἐκ τοῦ πονηροῦ. 16 ἐκ τοῦ κόσμου οὐκ εἰσὶν καθὼς ἐγὼ οὐκ εἰμὶ ἐκ τοῦ κόσμου. 17 ἁγίασον αὐτοὺς ἐν τῇ ἀληθείᾳ· ὁ λόγος ὁ σὸς ἀλήθειά ἐστιν. 18 καθὼς ἐμὲ ἀπέστειλας εἰς τὸν κόσμον, κἀγὼ ἀπέστειλα αὐτοὺς εἰς τὸν κόσμον· 19 καὶ ὑπὲρ αὐτῶν ἐγὼ ἁγιάζω ἐμαυτόν, ἵνα ὦσιν καὶ αὐτοὶ ἡγιασμένοι ἐν ἀληθείᾳ.
20 Οὐ περὶ τούτων δὲ ἐρωτῶ μόνον, ἀλλὰ καὶ περὶ τῶν πιστευόντων διὰ τοῦ λόγου αὐτῶν εἰς ἐμέ, 21 ἵνα πάντες ἓν ὦσιν, καθὼς σύ, πάτερ, ἐν ἐμοὶ κἀγὼ ἐν σοί, ἵνα καὶ αὐτοὶ ἐν ἡμῖν ὦσιν, ἵνα ὁ κόσμος πιστεύῃ ὅτι σύ με ἀπέστειλας. 22 κἀγὼ τὴν δόξαν ἣν δέδωκάς μοι δέδωκα αὐτοῖς, ἵνα ὦσιν ἓν καθὼς ἡμεῖς ἕν, 23 ἐγὼ ἐν αὐτοῖς καὶ σὺ ἐν ἐμοί, ἵνα ὦσιν τετελειωμένοι εἰς ἕν, ἵνα γινώσκῃ ὁ κόσμος ὅτι σύ με ἀπέστειλας καὶ ἠγάπησας αὐτοὺς καθὼς ἐμὲ ἠγάπησας. 24 πάτερ, ὃ δέδωκάς μοι, θέλω ἵνα ὅπου εἰμὶ ἐγὼ κἀκεῖνοι ὦσιν μετ᾽ ἐμοῦ, ἵνα θεωρῶσιν τὴν δόξαν τὴν ἐμὴν ἣν δέδωκάς μοι, ὅτι ἠγάπησάς με πρὸ καταβολῆς κόσμου. 25 Πάτερ δίκαιε, καὶ ὁ κόσμος σε οὐκ ἔγνω, ἐγὼ δέ σε ἔγνων, καὶ οὗτοι ἔγνωσαν ὅτι σύ με ἀπέστειλας, 26 καὶ ἐγνώρισα αὐτοῖς τὸ ὄνομά σου καὶ γνωρίσω, ἵνα ἡ ἀγάπη ἣν ἠγάπησάς με ἐν αὐτοῖς ᾖ κἀγὼ ἐν αὐτοῖς.

Chapter 18

18:1 Ταῦτα εἰπὼν Ἰησοῦς ἐξῆλθεν σὺν τοῖς μαθηταῖς αὐτοῦ πέραν τοῦ χειμάρρου τοῦ Κεδρὼν ὅπου ἦν κῆπος, εἰς ὃν εἰσῆλθεν αὐτὸς καὶ οἱ μαθηταὶ αὐτοῦ.

2 ᾔδει δὲ καὶ Ἰούδας ὁ παραδιδοὺς αὐτὸν τὸν τόπον, ὅτι πολλάκις συνήχθη Ἰησοῦς ἐκεῖ μετὰ τῶν μαθητῶν αὐτοῦ. 3 ὁ οὖν Ἰούδας λαβὼν τὴν σπεῖραν καὶ ἐκ τῶν ἀρχιερέων καὶ ἐκ τῶν Φαρισαίων ὑπηρέτας ἔρχεται ἐκεῖ μετὰ φανῶν καὶ λαμπάδων καὶ ὅπλων.

17:13 But now I am coming to you and I am speaking these things in the world, in order that they would have my joy fulfilled in themselves. 17:14 I myself have given them your word, and the world hated them, because they are not from the world, just as I myself am not from the world. 17:15 I am not requesting that you would take them from the world but that you would keep them from the evil one. 17:16 They are not from the world just as I myself am not from the world. 17:17 Sanctify them in the truth; your word is the truth. 17:18 Just as you sent me into the world, I myself also sent them into the world. 17:19 And for their sakes I myself am sanctifying myself, in order that they themselves also would be sanctified in the truth. 17:20 Not concerning these ones only am I asking, but also concerning the ones that are believing in me through their word, 17:21 in order that they would all be one, just as you, Father, are in me, and I in you, in order that they themselves also would be in us, in order that the world would believe that you yourself sent me. 17:22 And the glory which you have given to me, I myself have given to them, in order that they would be one, just as we are one, 17:23 I in them and you in me, in order that they would be perfected into one, in order that the world would know that you yourself sent me and loved them, just as you loved me. 17:24 Father, whom you have given to me, I desire that where I myself am, those ones would be with me, in order that they would behold my glory, which you have given to me, because you loved me before the foundation of the world. 17:25 O righteous Father, the world did not know you, but I myself knew you, and these ones knew that you yourself sent me; 17:26 and I made known to them your name and will make it known, in order that the love which you loved me would be in them, and I in them." 18:1 After speaking these words, Jesus went forth with his disciples over the Valley of Kidron where there was a garden, into which he himself entered, and his disciples. 18:2 Well, Judas, the one that betrayed him, also knew the place, because Jesus gathered there many times with his disciples. 18:3 Therefore, Judas, after taking the *Roman* cohort and officers from the chief priests and the Pharisees, goes there with lanterns and torches and weapons.

18:4–10

18:4 Jesus, therefore, knowing all the things that were coming upon him, went out, and says to them, "Whom are you seeking?" 18:5 They answered back to him, "Jesus the Nazarene." Jesus says to them, "I am." Moreover, Judas, the one that betrayed him, also stood with them. 18:6 Therefore, as he spoke to them, "I am," they went backward and fell to the ground. 18:7 Again, therefore, he asked them, "Whom are you seeking?" And they said, "Jesus the Nazarene." 18:8 Jesus answered back, "I told you that I am; if, therefore, you are seeking me, permit these ones to depart;" 18:9 in order that the word which he spoke, would be fulfilled, namely, this: "Those whom you have given to me, I did not lose a single one of them." 18:10 Simon Peter, therefore, having a sword, drew it and struck the high priest's servant and cut off his right ear. Moreover, the servant's name was Malchus.

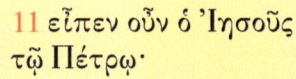
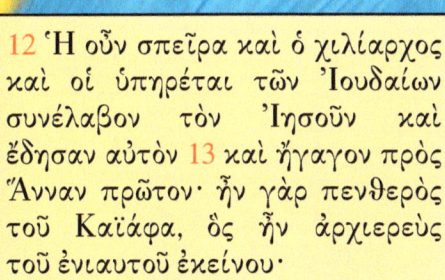

18:11 Jesus, therefore, said to Peter, "Put the sword into the sheath; the cup which the Father has given me, will I never ever drink it?"
18:12 Therefore, the *Roman* cohort and the commander and the officers of the Jewish Officials seized Jesus and bound him 18:13 and led him to Annas first; for he was father-in-law of Caiaphas, who was high priest during that year. 18:14 Additionally, Caiaphas was the one that had given counsel to the Jewish Officials that it was beneficial that one man die for the people. 18:15 Well, Simon Peter was following Jesus, and so was another disciple. Moreover, that disciple was known to the high priest and entered in with Jesus into the court of the high priest, 18:16 but Peter stood at the door outside. Therefore, the other disciple known to the high priest went out and spoke to the female doorkeeper and brought in Peter. 18:17 Therefore, the female servant doorkeeper says to Peter, "You yourself aren't also from the disciples of this person, are you?! (Surely not!)" That one says, "I am not." 18:18 Well, the servants and the officers stood having made a fire of coals, because it was cold and they were warming themselves. Moreover, Peter was also with them, standing and warming himself.

18:19–27

19 Ὁ οὖν ἀρχιερεὺς ἠρώτησεν τὸν Ἰησοῦν περὶ τῶν μαθητῶν αὐτοῦ καὶ περὶ τῆς διδαχῆς αὐτοῦ. 20 ἀπεκρίθη αὐτῷ Ἰησοῦς·

Ἐγὼ παρρησίᾳ λελάληκα τῷ κόσμῳ· ἐγὼ πάντοτε ἐδίδαξα ἐν συναγωγῇ καὶ ἐν τῷ ἱερῷ, ὅπου πάντες οἱ Ἰουδαῖοι συνέρχονται, καὶ ἐν κρυπτῷ ἐλάλησα οὐδέν·

21 τί με ἐρωτᾷς; ἐρώτησον τοὺς ἀκηκοότας τί ἐλάλησα αὐτοῖς· ἴδε οὗτοι οἴδασιν ἃ εἶπον ἐγώ.

22 ταῦτα δὲ αὐτοῦ εἰπόντος εἷς παρεστηκὼς τῶν ὑπηρετῶν ἔδωκεν ῥάπισμα τῷ Ἰησοῦ εἰπών·

Οὕτως ἀποκρίνῃ τῷ ἀρχιερεῖ;

23 ἀπεκρίθη αὐτῷ Ἰησοῦς·

Εἰ κακῶς ἐλάλησα, μαρτύρησον περὶ τοῦ κακοῦ· εἰ δὲ καλῶς, τί με δέρεις;

24 ἀπέστειλεν οὖν αὐτὸν ὁ Ἄννας δεδεμένον πρὸς Καϊάφαν τὸν ἀρχιερέα.

25 Ἦν δὲ Σίμων Πέτρος ἑστὼς καὶ θερμαινόμενος. εἶπον οὖν αὐτῷ·

Μὴ καὶ σὺ ἐκ τῶν μαθητῶν αὐτοῦ εἶ;

ἠρνήσατο ἐκεῖνος καὶ εἶπεν·

Οὐκ εἰμί.

26 λέγει εἷς ἐκ τῶν δούλων τοῦ ἀρχιερέως, συγγενὴς ὢν οὗ ἀπέκοψεν Πέτρος τὸ ὠτίον·

Οὐκ ἐγώ σε εἶδον ἐν τῷ κήπῳ μετ' αὐτοῦ;

27 πάλιν οὖν ἠρνήσατο Πέτρος· καὶ εὐθέως ἀλέκτωρ ἐφώνησεν.

18:19 Therefore, the high priest asked Jesus concerning his disciples and concerning his teaching. 18:20 Jesus answered back to him, "I myself have spoken candidly to the world; I myself always taught in synagogues and in the temple, where all the Jewish Officials regularly gather together, and I spoke nothing in secret. 18:21 Why are you questioning me? Question the ones that have heard what I spoke to them; look, these ones know the things which I myself spoke." 18:22 And after he said these things, one of the officers standing near gave Jesus a slap in the face, saying, "Are you answering back to the high priest in this way?!" 18:23 Jesus answered back to him, "If I have spoken badly, you testify concerning the bad; but if rightly, why do you hit me?" 18:24 Therefore, Annas sent him bound to Caiaphas the high priest. 18:25 Now Simon Peter was standing and warming himself. So, they said to him, "You yourself aren't also from his disciples, are you?! (Surely not!)" That one denied and said, "I am not." 18:26 One of the servants of the high priest, being a kinsman of the one whose ear Peter cut off, says, "Didn't I myself see you in the garden with him? (Yes!)" 18:27 Peter, therefore, denied it again; and immediately the cock crowed.

18:28 So, they lead Jesus from Caiaphas into the Praetorium. And it was early; and they themselves did not enter into the Praetorium, in order that they would not be defiled, but would eat the Passover. 18:29 Pilate, therefore, came outside to them and says, "What accusation are you bringing against this person?" 18:30 They answered back and said to him, "If this guy were not doing evil, we would not have delivered him up to you." 18:31 Pilate, therefore, said to them, "You yourselves take him and judge him according to your law." The Jewish Officials said to him, "It is not lawful for us to put any one to death"; 18:32 in order that the word of Jesus would be fulfilled, which he spoke, signifying by what manner of death he was going to die. 18:33 Pilate, therefore, entered again into the Praetorium and called Jesus and said to him, "Are you yourself the King of the Jews?" 18:34 Jesus answered back, "Do you yourself say this by your own accord or did others speak to you concerning me?" 18:35 Pilate answered back, "I'm not a Jew, am I? (No!) Your own nation and the chief priests delivered you to me; what did you do?" 18:36 Jesus answered back, "My kingdom is not from this world; if my kingdom were from this world, then my servants would be fighting, in order that I would not be delivered to the Jewish Officials; but now my kingdom is not from here." 18:37 Pilate, therefore, said to him, "Aren't you, therefore, a King?! (Surely yes!)"

18:37c–19:5

ἀπεκρίθη ὁ Ἰησοῦς·

Σὺ λέγεις ὅτι βασιλεύς εἰμι. ἐγὼ εἰς τοῦτο γεγέννημαι καὶ εἰς τοῦτο ἐλήλυθα εἰς τὸν κόσμον ἵνα μαρτυρήσω τῇ ἀληθείᾳ· πᾶς ὁ ὢν ἐκ τῆς ἀληθείας ἀκούει μου τῆς φωνῆς.

38 λέγει αὐτῷ ὁ Πιλᾶτος·

Τί ἐστιν ἀλήθεια;

Καὶ τοῦτο εἰπὼν πάλιν ἐξῆλθεν πρὸς τοὺς Ἰουδαίους, καὶ λέγει αὐτοῖς·

Ἐγὼ οὐδεμίαν εὑρίσκω ἐν αὐτῷ αἰτίαν· 39 ἔστιν δὲ συνήθεια ὑμῖν ἵνα ἕνα ἀπολύσω ὑμῖν ἐν τῷ πάσχα· βούλεσθε οὖν ἀπολύσω ὑμῖν τὸν βασιλέα τῶν Ἰουδαίων;

Μὴ τοῦτον ἀλλὰ τὸν Βαραββᾶν.

40 ἐκραύγασαν οὖν πάλιν λέγοντες·

ἦν δὲ ὁ Βαραββᾶς λῃστής.

Chapter 19

19:1 Τότε οὖν ἔλαβεν ὁ Πιλᾶτος τὸν Ἰησοῦν καὶ ἐμαστίγωσεν.

2 καὶ οἱ στρατιῶται πλέξαντες στέφανον ἐξ ἀκανθῶν ἐπέθηκαν αὐτοῦ τῇ κεφαλῇ,

καὶ ἱμάτιον πορφυροῦν περιέβαλον αὐτόν, 3 καὶ ἤρχοντο πρὸς αὐτὸν καὶ ἔλεγον·

Χαῖρε, ὁ βασιλεὺς τῶν Ἰουδαίων·

4 καὶ ἐξῆλθεν πάλιν ἔξω ὁ Πιλᾶτος καὶ λέγει αὐτοῖς·

Ἴδε ἄγω ὑμῖν αὐτὸν ἔξω, ἵνα γνῶτε ὅτι οὐδεμίαν αἰτίαν εὑρίσκω ἐν αὐτῷ.

5 ἐξῆλθεν οὖν ὁ Ἰησοῦς ἔξω, φορῶν τὸν ἀκάνθινον στέφανον καὶ τὸ πορφυροῦν ἱμάτιον. καὶ λέγει αὐτοῖς·

Ἰδοὺ ὁ ἄνθρωπος.

καὶ ἐδίδοσαν αὐτῷ ῥαπίσματα.

Jesus answered back, "You yourself say that I am a king. To this end I myself have been born and to this end I have come into the world, in order that I would bear witness to the truth. Every one that is from the truth hears my voice." 18:38 Pilate says to him, "What is truth?" And after saying this, he went out again to the Jewish Officials and says to them, "I myself am finding no crime in him. 18:39 But it is customary for you that I would release to you one person at the Passover; therefore, are you intending that I release to you the King of the Jews?" 18:40 Therefore, they cried out again, saying, "Not this one, but Barabbas!" Barabbas, however, was an insurrectionist! 19:1 Therefore, Pilate then took Jesus and scourged him. 19:2 And the soldiers, after weaving a crown from thorns, set it upon his head and dressed him in a purple garment; 19:3 and they kept coming to him and saying, "Hail, King of the Jews!" And they kept giving him slaps in the face. 19:4 And Pilate went outside again and says to them, "Look, I am bringing him outside to you, in order that you would know that I find no crime in him." 19:5 Jesus, therefore, went outside wearing the crown of thorns and the purple garment. And he says to them, "Behold, the person!"

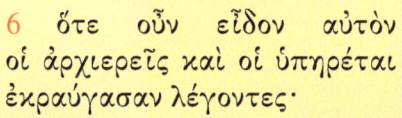
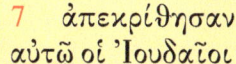
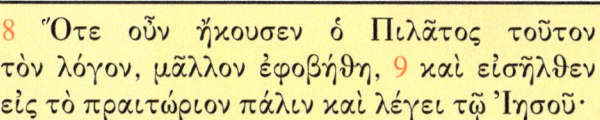

19:6 When, therefore, the chief priests and the officers saw him, they cried out saying, "Crucify, crucify!" Pilate says to them, "You yourselves take him and crucify him, for I myself find no crime in him!" 19:7 The Jewish Officials answered back to him, "We ourselves have a law and by that law he ought to die, because he made himself the Son of God." 19:8 Therefore, when Pilate heard this word, he was more afraid, 19:9 and he entered into the Praetorium again and says to Jesus, "Where are you yourself from?" Yet, Jesus gave him no answer. 19:10 Pilate, therefore, says to him, "Are you not speaking to me? You know, don't you, that I have authority to release you and I have authority to crucify you? (Surely, yes.)" 19:11 Jesus answered back to him, "You would have no authority against me unless it were given to you from above; for this reason, the one that delivered me to you has greater sin." 19:12 From this moment, Pilate began seeking to release him; but the Jewish Officials cried out, saying, "If you release this man, you are not a friend of Caesar's; every one that makes himself a king speaks against Caesar." 19:13 Therefore, Pilate, after hearing these words, brought Jesus outside and sat down on the judgment-seat at a place called 'The Pavement,' but in Hebrew, 'Gabbatha.' 19:14 Moreover, it was the preparation of the Passover; it was about the sixth hour. And he says to the Jewish Officials, "Look, your King!" 19:15 They, therefore, cried out, "Away, away! Crucify him!"

19:21 Therefore, the chief priests of the Jews kept saying to Pilate, "Do not write, 'The King of the Jews', but that that one said, 'I am King of the Jews.'" 19:22 Pilate answered back, "That which I have written I have written." 19:23 The soldiers, therefore, when they crucified Jesus, took his garments and made four parts, a portion for each soldier, and the tunic. Now the tunic was seamless, woven from the top throughout. 19:24 Therefore, they said to one another, "Let us not tear it but cast lots concerning whose it would be;" in order that the Scripture would be fulfilled that says, "They divided my clothing among themselves, and for my cloak they cast lots." These things, therefore, the soldiers did. 19:25 Well, by the cross of Jesus stood his mother and his mother's sister, Mary the wife of Clopas, and Mary Magdalene.

19:26 Therefore, Jesus, after seeing his mother and the disciple whom he loved standing by, says to his mother, "Woman, look, your son!" 19:27 Next he says to the disciple, "Look, your mother!" And from that hour, the disciple took her for his own. 19:28 After this, Jesus, knowing already that all things had been finished, in order that the Scripture would be fulfilled, says, "I am thirsty." 19:29 A vessel full of vinegar was lying there; so, putting a sponge full of the vinegar on a hyssop branch, they lifted it to his mouth.

30 ὅτε οὖν ἔλαβεν τὸ ὄξος ὁ Ἰησοῦς εἶπεν· Τετέλεσται, καὶ κλίνας τὴν κεφαλὴν παρέδωκεν τὸ πνεῦμα.

31 Οἱ οὖν Ἰουδαῖοι, ἐπεὶ παρασκευὴ ἦν, ἵνα μὴ μείνῃ ἐπὶ τοῦ σταυροῦ τὰ σώματα ἐν τῷ σαββάτῳ, ἦν γὰρ μεγάλη ἡ ἡμέρα ἐκείνου τοῦ σαββάτου, ἠρώτησαν τὸν Πιλᾶτον ἵνα κατεαγῶσιν αὐτῶν τὰ σκέλη καὶ ἀρθῶσιν. 32 ἦλθον οὖν οἱ στρατιῶται, καὶ τοῦ μὲν πρώτου κατέαξαν τὰ σκέλη καὶ τοῦ ἄλλου τοῦ συσταυρωθέντος αὐτῷ· 33 ἐπὶ δὲ τὸν Ἰησοῦν ἐλθόντες, ὡς εἶδον ἤδη αὐτὸν τεθνηκότα, οὐ κατέαξαν αὐτοῦ τὰ σκέλη, 34 ἀλλ᾽ εἷς τῶν στρατιωτῶν λόγχῃ αὐτοῦ τὴν πλευρὰν ἔνυξεν, καὶ ἐξῆλθεν εὐθὺς αἷμα καὶ ὕδωρ. 35 καὶ ὁ ἑωρακὼς μεμαρτύρηκεν, καὶ ἀληθινὴ αὐτοῦ ἐστιν ἡ μαρτυρία, καὶ ἐκεῖνος οἶδεν ὅτι ἀληθῆ λέγει, ἵνα καὶ ὑμεῖς πιστεύητε. 36 ἐγένετο γὰρ ταῦτα ἵνα ἡ γραφὴ πληρωθῇ·

Ὀστοῦν οὐ συντριβήσεται αὐτοῦ.

37 καὶ πάλιν ἑτέρα γραφὴ λέγει·

Ὄψονται εἰς ὃν ἐξεκέντησαν.

19:30 Therefore, when he received the vinegar, Jesus said, "It is finished." And lowering his head he gave up his spirit. **19:31** Therefore, the Jewish Officials, since it was the Preparation, in order that the bodies would not remain on the cross on the Sabbath (for the day of that Sabbath was a high day), asked Pilate that their legs would be broken and they would be taken away. **19:32** Therefore, the soldiers came and broke the legs of the first and of the other one that was crucified with him; **19:33** but when they came to Jesus, as they saw that he was already dead, they did not break his legs, **19:34** but one of the soldiers pierced his side with a spear, and immediately blood and water came out. **19:35** And the one that has seen has given testimony, and his witness is true, and that one knows that he is speaking the truth, in order that you yourselves would also believe. **19:36** For these things came to pass, in order that the Scripture would be fulfilled, "A bone of his will not be broken." **19:37** And again another Scripture says, "They will look to him whom they pierced."

19:38–20:2

38 Μετὰ δὲ ταῦτα ἠρώτησεν τὸν Πιλᾶτον Ἰωσὴφ ἀπὸ Ἁριμαθαίας, ὢν μαθητὴς τοῦ Ἰησοῦ κεκρυμμένος δὲ διὰ τὸν φόβον τῶν Ἰουδαίων, ἵνα ἄρῃ τὸ σῶμα τοῦ Ἰησοῦ· καὶ ἐπέτρεψεν ὁ Πιλᾶτος. ἦλθεν οὖν καὶ ἦρεν τὸ σῶμα αὐτοῦ.

39 ἦλθεν δὲ καὶ Νικόδημος, ὁ ἐλθὼν πρὸς αὐτὸν νυκτὸς τὸ πρῶτον, φέρων μίγμα σμύρνης καὶ ἀλόης ὡς λίτρας ἑκατόν. 40 ἔλαβον οὖν τὸ σῶμα τοῦ Ἰησοῦ καὶ ἔδησαν αὐτὸ ὀθονίοις μετὰ τῶν ἀρωμάτων, καθὼς ἔθος ἐστὶν τοῖς Ἰουδαίοις ἐνταφιάζειν.

41 ἦν δὲ ἐν τῷ τόπῳ ὅπου ἐσταυρώθη κῆπος, καὶ ἐν τῷ κήπῳ μνημεῖον καινόν, ἐν ᾧ οὐδέπω οὐδεὶς ἦν τεθειμένος· 42 ἐκεῖ οὖν διὰ τὴν παρασκευὴν τῶν Ἰουδαίων, ὅτι ἐγγὺς ἦν τὸ μνημεῖον, ἔθηκαν τὸν Ἰησοῦν.

Chapter 20

20:1 Τῇ δὲ μιᾷ τῶν σαββάτων Μαρία ἡ Μαγδαληνὴ ἔρχεται πρωῒ σκοτίας ἔτι οὔσης εἰς τὸ μνημεῖον, καὶ βλέπει τὸν λίθον ἠρμένον ἐκ τοῦ μνημείου.

2 τρέχει οὖν καὶ ἔρχεται πρὸς Σίμωνα Πέτρον καὶ πρὸς τὸν ἄλλον μαθητὴν ὃν ἐφίλει ὁ Ἰησοῦς, καὶ λέγει αὐτοῖς·

Ἦραν τὸν κύριον ἐκ τοῦ μνημείου, καὶ οὐκ οἴδαμεν ποῦ ἔθηκαν αὐτόν.

19:38 Then, after these things, Joseph from Arimathaea, being a disciple of Jesus but secretly out of fear of the Jewish Officials, asked Pilate in order that he might take away the body of Jesus; and Pilate permitted. Therefore, he came and took away his body. 19:39 Moreover, Nicodemus also came, the one that first came to him by night, bringing a mixture of myrrh and aloes, about a hundred pounds. 19:40 So they took the body of Jesus and clothed it in linen cloths with the spices, just as was the custom for the Jews to prepare for burial. 19:41 Moreover, there was in the place where he was crucified a garden, and in the garden a new tomb, in which a single person had not yet been placed. 19:42 So, on account of the Preparation of the Jews (because the tomb was near), they placed Jesus there. 20:1 Additionally, on the first day of the week, Mary Magdalene comes early, while it was yet dark, to the tomb, and sees the stone taken away from the tomb. 20:2 Therefore, she runs and comes to Simon Peter and to the other disciple (whom Jesus continuously loved) and says to them, "They took away the Lord from the tomb and we do not know where they placed him."

3 ἐξῆλθεν οὖν ὁ Πέτρος καὶ ὁ ἄλλος μαθητής, καὶ ἤρχοντο εἰς τὸ μνημεῖον. 4 ἔτρεχον δὲ οἱ δύο ὁμοῦ· καὶ ὁ ἄλλος μαθητὴς προέδραμεν τάχιον τοῦ Πέτρου καὶ ἦλθεν πρῶτος εἰς τὸ μνημεῖον, 5 καὶ παρακύψας βλέπει κείμενα τὰ ὀθόνια, οὐ μέντοι εἰσῆλθεν.

6 ἔρχεται οὖν καὶ Σίμων Πέτρος ἀκολουθῶν αὐτῷ, καὶ εἰσῆλθεν εἰς τὸ μνημεῖον· καὶ θεωρεῖ τὰ ὀθόνια κείμενα,

7 καὶ τὸ σουδάριον, ὃ ἦν ἐπὶ τῆς κεφαλῆς αὐτοῦ, οὐ μετὰ τῶν ὀθονίων κείμενον ἀλλὰ χωρὶς ἐντετυλιγμένον εἰς ἕνα τόπον· 8 τότε οὖν εἰσῆλθεν καὶ ὁ ἄλλος μαθητὴς ὁ ἐλθὼν πρῶτος εἰς τὸ μνημεῖον, καὶ εἶδεν καὶ ἐπίστευσεν· 9 οὐδέπω γὰρ ᾔδεισαν τὴν γραφὴν ὅτι δεῖ αὐτὸν ἐκ νεκρῶν ἀναστῆναι.

10 ἀπῆλθον οὖν πάλιν πρὸς αὐτοὺς οἱ μαθηταί. 11 Μαρία δὲ εἱστήκει πρὸς τῷ μνημείῳ ἔξω κλαίουσα. ὡς οὖν ἔκλαιεν παρέκυψεν εἰς τὸ μνημεῖον, 12 καὶ θεωρεῖ δύο ἀγγέλους ἐν λευκοῖς καθεζομένους, ἕνα πρὸς τῇ κεφαλῇ καὶ ἕνα πρὸς τοῖς ποσίν, ὅπου ἔκειτο τὸ σῶμα τοῦ Ἰησοῦ.

13 καὶ λέγουσιν αὐτῇ ἐκεῖνοι·

Γύναι, τί κλαίεις;

20:3 Peter, therefore, went forth, and the other disciple, and they were going to the tomb. 20:4 Moreover, the two were running together; and the other disciple ran ahead faster than Peter and came first to the tomb, 20:5 and stooping to look, he sees the linen cloths lying there, although he did not enter. 20:6 So, Simon Peter also comes, following him, and he entered into the tomb; and he beholds the linen cloths lying there, 20:7 and the facecloth, which was upon his head, not lying with the linen cloths, but rolled up separately in a single place. 20:8 Then, therefore, the other disciple also entered, the one that came first to the tomb, and he saw and believed. 20:9 For they did not yet know the Scripture that he must rise from the dead. 20:10 Therefore, the disciples departed again to themselves. 20:11 But Mary stood at the tomb outside weeping. Therefore, as she was weeping, she stooped to look into the tomb, 20:12 and she beholds two angels in white sitting, one at the head, and one at the feet, where the body of Jesus was placed. 20:13 and those ones say to her, "Woman, why are you weeping?"

20:13c She says to them this: "They have taken away my Lord and I do not know where they placed him." 20:14 After saying these things, she turned backwards and beholds Jesus standing and did not know that it was Jesus. 20:15 Jesus says to her, "Woman, why are you weeping? Whom are you seeking?" That woman, supposing that he was the gardener, says to him, "Sir, if you yourself carried him, tell me where you placed him and I myself will take him away." 20:16 Jesus says to her, "Mary!" After turning, that woman says to him in Hebrew, "Rabboni!" (which is to say, 'Teacher.') 20:17 Jesus says to her, "Don't keep holding me, for I am not yet ascended to the Father! But go to my brothers and say to them, 'I am ascending to my Father and your Father, and my God and your God.' 20:18 Mary Magdalene goes, reporting to the disciples this: "I have seen the Lord" and that he spoke these things to her.

20:19–26

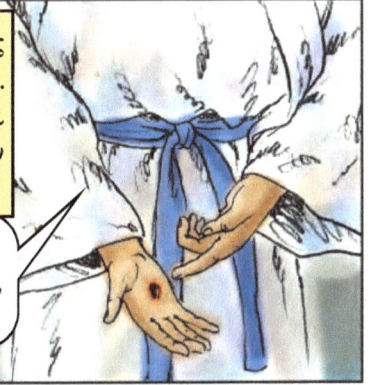

20:19 Therefore, while it was evening on that day, the first day of the week, and when the doors had been shut where the disciples were for fear of the Jewish Officials, Jesus came and stood in the middle, and says to them, "Peace to you!" 20:20 And after saying this, he showed his hands and his side to them. Therefore, the disciples rejoiced having seen the Lord. 20:21 Jesus, therefore, said to them again, "Peace to you! Just as the Father sent me, I also am sending you." 20:22 And after saying this, he breathed upon and says to them, "Receive the Holy Spirit: 20:23 if you forgive the sins of some, they are forgiven for them; if you hold them, they have been held." 20:24 Now Thomas, one from the twelve, the one called Didymus, was not with them when Jesus came. 20:25 Therefore, the other disciples kept saying to him, "We have seen the Lord!" But he said to them, "Unless I see in his hands the place of the nails and put my finger into the place of the nails and put my hand into his side, I will never ever believe." 20:26 And after eight days again his disciples were inside, and Thomas with them. Jesus comes, with the doors having been shut, and stood in the middle and said, "Peace to you!"

20:27–21:3

20:27 Then he says to Thomas, "Bring your finger here and look at see my hands; and bring your hand and put it into my side, and don't be unbelieving, but believing!" 20:28 Thomas answered back and said to him, "My Lord and my God!" 20:29 Jesus says to him, "Because you have seen me, you have believed? Blessed are the ones that have not seen and believe!" 20:30 Therefore, then, Jesus also accomplished many other signs in the presence of the disciples, which are not written in this book; 20:31 but, these have been written, in order that you would believe that Jesus is the Anointed One, the Son of God, and that by believing you would have life in his name. 21:1 After these things Jesus manifested himself again to the disciples at the sea of Tiberius; and he manifested himself in this way. 21:2 They were together, Simon Peter and Thomas, the one called Didymus, and Nathanael of Cana in Galilee, and the sons of Zebedee, and two other of his disciples. 21:3 Simon Peter says to them, "I departing to go fishing." They say to him, "We ourselves are also coming with you." They went forth and entered into the boat and on that night they caught nothing.

21:4 But after dawn had already come, Jesus stood on the beach, although the disciples did not know that it was Jesus. 21:5 Jesus, therefore, says to them, "Children, you don't have something to eat, do you? (No.)" They answered back to him, "No." 21:6 And he said to them, "Cast the net on the right side of the boat, and you will find something." Therefore, they cast and they were strong enough to haul it up from the multitude of fishes. 21:7 Therefore, that disciple whom Jesus loved, says to Peter, "It is the Lord." So, Simon Peter, after hearing that it was the Lord, put on his outer garment (for he was naked) and threw himself into the sea. 21:8 But the other disciples came in the little boat (for they were not far from the land but about two hundred cubits off), dragging the net full of fishes. 21:9 Therefore, as they got out upon the land, they see a fire of coals lying there and fish lying upon it and bread. 21:10 Jesus says to them, "Bring in from the fish which you have now taken." 21:11 Simon Peter, therefore, went up and drew the net onto the land, full of great fishes, a hundred and fifty and three; and although being such a large quantity of these, the net was not ripped.

21:12 Jesus says to them, "Come, eat breakfast!" And none of the disciples was daring to question him, "Who are you?" knowing that it was the Lord. 21:13 Jesus comes and takes the bread and gives it to them, and the fish likewise. 21:14 This already was the third time Jesus was manifested to the disciples, after being raised from the dead. 21:15 So, when they had broken their fast, Jesus says to Simon Peter, "Simon, son of John, do you love me more than these?" He says to him, "Yes, Lord; you know that I love you!" He says to him, "Feed my lambs!" 21:16 He says to him again, a second time, "Simon, son of John, do you love me?" He says to him, "Yes, Lord; you know that I love you!" He says to him, "Tend my sheep!" 21:17 He says to him the third time, "Simon, son of John, do you love me?" And Peter was grieved that he had spoken to him the third time, "Do you love me?" And he said to him, "Lord, you yourself know all things; you yourself know that I love you!" Jesus says to him, "Feed my sheep! 21:18 Amen! Amen! I say to you, when you were young, you were clothing yourself and walking where you wanted; but when you are old, you will stretch forth your hands, and another will dress you and carry you where you do not want." 21:19 Well, he spoke this, signifying by what manner of death he would glorify God.

21:19b And after speaking this, he says to him, "Follow me!" 21:20 Peter, turning about, sees the disciple whom Jesus loved following, who also leaned back upon his breast at the supper, and said, "Lord, who is the one that betrays you?" 21:21 Therefore, after seeing this one, Peter says to Jesus, "Lord, and what about this one?" 21:22 Jesus says to him, "If I want him to remain until I come, what is that to you? You yourself follow me!" 21:23 Therefore, this word went forth to the brothers that that disciple does not die. Yet, Jesus did not say to him that he does not die, but, "If I want him to remain until I come, what is that to you?!" 21:24 This is the disciple that bears witness concerning these things and that wrote these things, and we know that his testimony is true. 21:25 Furthermore, there are also many other things which Jesus did, which if each one is ever written down, I don't suppose that even the world itself would have room enough for the written books.

Check Out These & Other Great Resources At
GlossaHouse.com

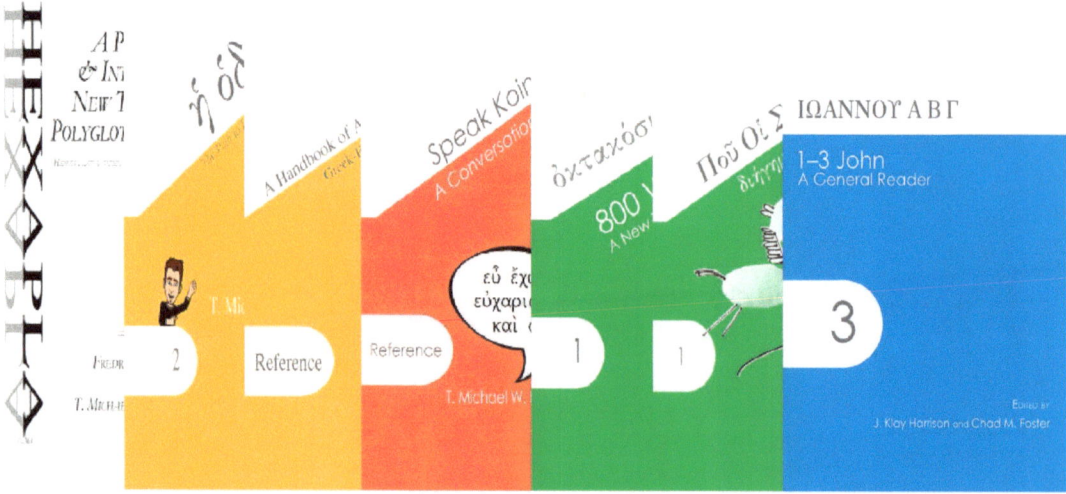

A Parallel & Interlinear New Testament Polyglot: Luke-Acts | The Path to Learning Greek | A Handbook of Ancient Greek Grammatical Terms | Speak Koine Greek | 800 Words and Images | 1-3 John: A General Reader

Learn More About The First Ever Ancient Greek Honor Society, Gamma Rho Kappa, And How You Or Your Institution Can Join Or Start A Chapter Today.

Visit GlossaHouse.com For More Details.

Learn More About The Artwork, Design, & Illustration Projects of Keith R. Neely Directly At KeithRNeely@comcast.com. Also Visit FreeIllustratedBible.com.

Look For More Volumes In The GlossaHouse Illustrated Greek-English New Testament With Illustrations By Keith R. Neely.

www.ingramcontent.com/pod-product-compliance
Lightning Source LLC
Chambersburg PA
CBHW041523220426
43669CB00003B/37